MOMENTS *of* PEACE
for a WOMAN'S HEART

PRESENTED TO

PRESENTED BY

DATE

MOMENTS *of* PEACE *for a* WOMAN'S HEART

MOMENTS
of PEACE
for a
WOMAN'S
HEART

Reflections of
God's Gifts of Love,
Hope, and Comfort

BETHANY HOUSE
MINNEAPOLIS, MINNESOTA

Moments of Peace for a Woman's Heart
Copyright ©2008 by GRQ Inc.

Published by Bethany House Publishers
11400 Hampshire Avenue South
Bloomington, Minnesota 55438

Bethany House Publishers is a division of Baker Publishing Group, Grand Rapids, Michigan.

ISBN 978-0-7642-0550-7

Editor: Teri Wilhelms
Associate Editor: Natasha Sperling
Manuscript written and prepared by Rebecca Currington & the Snapdragon Group
Design: Diane Whisner

10 11 12 13 — 5 4 3 2

CONTENTS

INTRODUCTION

Would you be surprised to learn that God loves you? He does! He loves you with all his heart, and he knows you better than you know yourself. That's because you are his creation, his handiwork, the expression of his artistic genius. He knows about your struggles and your achievements. He knows about your secret acts of kindness and your secret sins. He knows what you need and what you don't need. He knows, and he wants you to know too—both who you are and who he is.

Moments of Peace for a Woman's Heart was written for that purpose. It opens the door wide to knowing God and becoming the woman he created you to be. When you look into his face and see your reflection in his loving eyes, you'll receive strength to overcome fears and obstacles, discover new ways of thinking, and develop the skills to walk in new and exciting paths.

It is our prayer that as you read, you will see and understand God's wonderful plan for you, a plan designed to reveal your incredible worth and beauty. In seeking, you will find more treasure than you ever imagined.

Knowing

SOMEONE WORTH KNOWING

Skilled living gets its start in the Fear-of-God,
insight into life from knowing a Holy God.
PROVERBS 9:10 MSG

Imagine that you've made a new friend. You want to learn all about the new person in your life. You can't wait for conversations to begin.

God is also a friend worth knowing. Unlike the wooden statues some worship, he is accessible. He wants to be known. He's told you all about himself in his Word, and he waits enthusiastically for the dialogue to begin.

If your heart longs to know him, to grasp who he really is and what he wants from you, sit down with an open heart and an open Bible and get to know the God of the universe, who loves you with an everlasting love.

Wonderful Father: Thank you for reaching out to me and
opening the door to a loving, everlasting relationship
between the two of us. Thank you for allowing
me to know you. Amen.

Thanks be to God, who in Christ always leads us in triumphal procession, and through us spreads in every place the fragrance that comes from knowing him.

2 CORINTHIANS 2:14 NRSV

UNPARALLELED GREATNESS

Shout aloud and sing for joy, people of Zion, for great is the Holy One of Israel among you.

ISAIAH 12:6 NIV

You have a powerful friend. He is more powerful than any world leader. There's no chance that he will ever be

voted out of office or forced off his throne. His reign is eternal; his greatness unparalleled. He has placed a million suns in the reaches of space and fixed the planets in their magnificent orbits. This great and wonderful God cares about you.

You may never fully understand the extent of your good fortune, but it is yours just the same, along with all the benefits that come with knowing such a mighty God. Rejoice. All things are possible for you.

*Dear God: I am in awe of your power and majesty and humbled that someone like you would want me.
I reach for your extended hand. Amen.*

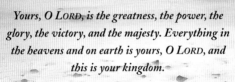

*Yours, O L*ORD*, is the greatness, the power, the glory, the victory, and the majesty. Everything in the heavens and on earth is yours, O L*ORD*, and this is your kingdom.*

1 CHRONICLES **29:11** NLT

PERFECT IN EVERY WAY

*The LORD is righteous in all His ways,
gracious in all His works.*

PSALM 145:17 NKJV

In the world we live in, it is said that absolute power corrupts absolutely. This is not so with God. His ways are always right—wise, just, and free of any wrong. Know that he will always do what's best for you. He will never fail you, and he will never abandon you. He will only bring goodness to your life.

As you open your heart to him, his nature will change your life. You will begin to see things differently and more clearly. Wrong thoughts will be swept away by good thoughts. Your actions will follow as you come to know God and become more and more like him.

Merciful Father: I desire that my thoughts and actions be right, just as you are. Thank you for seeing me as I should be rather than as I am. Amen.

*I am the LORD; I act with steadfast love, jus-
tice, and righteousness in the earth, for in
these things I delight, says the LORD.*

JEREMIAH 9:24 NRSV

AT HIS WORD

I will come and proclaim your mighty acts,
O Sovereign LORD; I will proclaim your
righteousness, yours alone.

PSALM 71:16 NIV

Would anyone serve a god who is weak and easily manipulated, one without authority? You would not be serving a god at all. The God of the Bible is sovereign, the holder of ultimate authority. At his word, the heavens came into being. At his word, you came into being. He is the author,

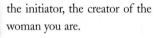 the initiator, the creator of the woman you are.

Does it surprise you to learn that God knows you so well and still loves you so much? He does! He can't be talked into changing his mind. He simply chooses to love you, and by his mighty Word, he promises that will never change.

Dear God: Thank you for loving me just as
I am. May I walk in humble submission
to your power and will. Amen.

*I look to you for help, O Sovereign
LORD. You are my refuge.*

PSALM 141:8 NLT

THE MIGHTY JUDGE

*The Lord is still in his holy temple; he still rules
from heaven. He closely watches everything
that happens here on earth*

PSALM 11:4 TLB

It's easy to feel powerless in this world, especially if
you're a woman. But when you place your trust in God,

you can stand strong and confident,
knowing you have a friend and advo-
cate in the highest of places. It is
someone who is looking out for your
interests, someone who is perfectly
just and steadfastly good.

You need not accept quietly everything that life lays at your feet. Lift up
your eyes to heaven. Plead your case before the mighty
judge of all. He loves you, and because of that, you can be
sure he will hear you and do what is best for you.

*Loving Father: I bring my cause before you today.
I place it in your hands, and I thank you for
providing a place of rest for me. Amen.*

True wisdom and real power belong to God;
from him we learn how to live.

ISAIAH **30:18** MSG

DRAWING FROM THE WELL

God is the real source of wisdom and strength.
JOB 12:13 CEV

What if you could go each morning and draw wisdom
and strength from a pure and bottomless well? No matter how depleted you might feel as you close your eyes at

night, you would know that you would
soon be refreshed and replenished.
There really is a well just like that.

God invites you to come to him each
day, to draw from his never-ending
supply of wisdom and strength. His
resources are endless, and he's promised never to deny you when you ask

for his help. He's always there waiting, ready to give you
what you need to take on another day with grace and
confidence.

Heavenly Father: I need a fresh drink of your wisdom
each day. Thank you for inviting me to
come and be refreshed. Amen.

*Oh, what a wonderful God we have! How great
are his riches and wisdom and knowledge.*

ROMANS 11:33 NLT

THE REAL THING

Jesus said, "No one is good but One, that is, God."
MATTHEW 19:17 NKJV

As children we were admonished to be good, to mind our manners, to play by the rules, and to see to the needs of others. But at some point in every woman's life, she real-

izes that as hard as she tries, she can only do so much. She will never be able to be good in the eyes of everyone.

Each woman must come to understand that pure goodness comes from God. It is woven inextricably into his very nature, the essence of who he really is. When you enter into relationship with him, he shares his unblemished nature with you and urges you to keep your eyes on him rather than on the expectations of others.

Dear God: You know that I have always tried to be good. As I get to know you, place your pure goodness in my heart. Amen.

O taste and see that the LORD is good.

PSALM 34:8 NRSV

FULLY ACCEPTED

*There is neither Jew nor Greek, there is neither
slave nor free man, there is neither male nor female;
for you are all one in Christ Jesus.*

GALATIANS 3:28 NASB

Every woman knows that in this world not everyone is
treated equally. It's a lesson she will learn again and

again on her path through life.
God has instituted a different
standard in his kingdom; there
are no distinctions, we all have
equal standing before him.

What a wonderful thought to
ponder. There are no limitations on your relationship with
God. Your earthly social and cultural standing are of no
importance to him. Your gender, your age, and your
parentage are of no consequence to the ruler of heaven
and earth. He accepts you fully and completely as you
are. You can count on that.

*Dear God: Thank you for seeing past all the extraneous
criteria by which I am defined and accepting me
completely for who I am. Amen.*

He destined us for adoption as his children through Jesus Christ, according to the good pleasure of his will ... his glorious grace that he freely bestowed on us.

EPHESIANS 1:5–6 NRSV

THE MERCIFUL FATHER

God … does not retain His anger forever,
because He delights in unchanging love.

MICAH 7:18 NASB

Mercy is difficult to define, but we've all experienced it.
Mercy saves and redeems and preserves all that it touches.
It is like rain that falls on a parched desert and brings forth
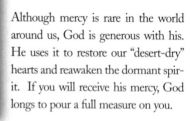 a multitude of new blossoms.

Although mercy is rare in the world
around us, God is generous with his.
He uses it to restore our "desert-dry"
hearts and reawaken the dormant spirit. If you will receive his mercy, God
longs to pour a full measure on you.

If you find that your spirit is in need of the restoration
that God's mercy can bring, reach out to him. You will
receive all that you need.

Dear God: I need your mercy to bring life back to the
desert in my heart. Thank you for giving your
mercy to me freely and generously. Amen.

The Lord is compassionate and merciful.

JAMES 5:11 NRSV

THE GREATEST LOVE OF ALL

Yes, I have loved you with an everlasting love.
JEREMIAH 31:3 NKJV

Think about what you love most in the world. Now try to multiply that love by infinity. The human mind cannot contain such a concept. In the same way, we cannot

even begin to comprehend the magnitude of God's love for us. It's a love that will last forever, and it remains unchanged in the face of our mistakes, unaltered by time or circumstances.

You have probably been looking for such a love all your life. You may think you don't deserve to be loved so deeply and unconditionally. The fact is that God's love is not limited by our small thinking. God, who knows you best, loves you most.

Heavenly Father: I can't comprehend the depths of your love for me. But I receive it with a grateful heart. Amen.

How precious is Your lovingkindness, O God!
And the children of men take refuge in the
shadow of Your wings.

PSALM 36:7 NASB

HE IS WAITING

You, the LORD God, are kind and merciful.
You don't easily get angry, and your
love can always be trusted.

PSALM 86:15 CEV

Someone is waiting for you—it's God! And he's determined to wait as long as it takes. As long as you have

breath, he will be there, hoping that
you will turn your face to him and
return his love for you. He is patient
and forgiving.

He doesn't care if you've ignored him
in the past or even rejected him. Like
a father longing for the return of his
wayward child, he never gives up
hope. And should you turn to him, he will not throw the
past at you. He will simply say, "Welcome home, my
beautiful child. I have been waiting."

Dear God: Thank you for patiently waiting
for me, for never giving up, and for receiving
me without any reservation. Amen.

*The Lord is slow to anger, and
abounding in steadfast love.*

NUMBERS **14:18** NRSV

THE GOD OF SECOND CHANCES

*The LORD helps the fallen and lifts up
those bent beneath their loads.*

PSALM 145:14 NLT

It would be great if we could live our lives perfectly,
always making good, appropriate choices. We can't,

because we have free will—a priceless
gift from God. He wants us to have a
loving relationship with him because we
choose to, not because we were
designed to.

The risk of free will is we often choose
wrongly. God knew we would and paid
for our mistakes ahead of time. In
return, he only wants us to ask to be forgiven. He has
promised not to deny our request. Why be burdened
with your mistakes? You can lay them down at the feet
of the God of Second Chances.

*Heavenly Father: Thank you for freely granting me
the right to choose. And forgive me for the
wrong choices I have made. Amen.*

Lord, you are kind and forgiving and have
great love for those who call to you.

PSALM 86:5 NCV

HE WILL NEVER FAIL YOU

*Let us hold unswervingly to the hope we profess,
for he who promised is faithful.*

HEBREWS 10:23 NIV

All people fail at one time or another. The best-laid plans can come up short. God will never fail you. He is  the one constant in your life that you can trust, utterly and without reservation.

You won't have to wonder if he'll be there tomorrow or if he will still love you. He will. You can count on that and on all the other promises God has made to you in the Bible—more than 5,000 in all. Though he may not do things in the way you expect, you can be certain that he will never, ever let you down. He is faithful.

*Dear Father: I place my heart in your hands and
my trust in your faithfulness. Thank you for
always being there for me. Amen.*

The LORD is faithful in all his words,
and gracious in all his deeds.

PSALM 145:13 NRSV

HIS COMFORTING HAND

I serve you, LORD. Comfort me with your love,
just as you have promised.

PSALM 119:76 CEV

As women, we spend a lot of time comforting others.
But what happens when we need to be comforted? God

is always there, reaching out
his hand, calming us, reassur-
ing us, loving us.

You need only to place yourself in God's strong, capable
hands. Maybe you need to feel

his presence alongside you when your spirit is tested by
grief or sorrow. Is your body aching or your troubled
mind screaming for relief? God is there for you—today,
tomorrow, and the next day. Do not be afraid to cry out
to him. The Bible says your tears are precious to him. Let
him comfort you.

Dear God: I have no one to turn to but you.
Thank you for never leaving my side in
the good times and the bad. Amen.

You keep track of all my sorrows. You have collected all my tears in your bottle. You have recorded each one in your book.

PSALM 56:8 NLT

Seeking

LOOK AND SEE

It is not those who commend themselves that are approved, but those whom the Lord commends.

2 CORINTHIANS 10:18 NRSV

Some women spend a considerable amount of time in front of the mirror each morning, while others may only take a quick glance at themselves before dashing out the

door. Perhaps you're somewhere in between. No matter the way or how long you look at yourself, God is the one who sees you clearly.

God sees and appreciates your true inner beauty that the mir-

ror doesn't reveal. Because of his unconditional love for you, you need never worry about being enough, doing enough, or achieving enough to earn his approval. You already have it.

Look in the mirror. Ask God to show you the beloved and beautiful woman he sees.

Dear God: You know me better than I know myself, and you love me. Let me see myself through the eyes of your love. Amen.

*The L*ORD *does not look at the things man looks at.*
Man looks at the outward appearance,
*but the L*ORD *looks at the heart.*

1 SAMUEL **16:7** NIV

A NEW BEGINNING

*God, make a fresh start in me, shape a
Genesis week from the chaos of my life.*

PSALM 51:10 MSG

Choices and decisions of all kinds confront us on our
life's journey, and sometimes we make mistakes. It has
nothing to do with being a woman, and everything to do
 with being human. That's why
God does something about our
human mistakes. He forgives
them. He gives us not only a clean
heart but also a fresh start.

Perhaps you feel guilty for something you have said or done. No
matter how serious it may have been, God waits for you
with open arms. He stands ready to dry your tears, forgive you, and comfort you. Let him give you a new
beginning.

*Dear Father: Help me find peace in
your forgiveness. Show me the way to
a new beginning in my life. Amen.*

*I will give you a new heart and
put a new spirit within you.*

EZEKIEL 36:26 NKJV

LOOK FORWARD

*Forgetting the past and straining toward what is ahead,
I keep trying to reach the goal and get the prize for
which God called me through Christ to the life above.*

PHILIPPIANS 3:13–14 NCV

"The past cannot be changed," a woman once remarked.
"We have only today to make things happen." While

well aware of the hold the past
can exert over the present, the
woman reflected God's wisdom
in pointing us forward.

What keeps you looking back?
Do hurts, regrets, or grievances
from the past take your eyes away from today? If so, let
God show you how to let go. Let God help you leave
behind the negative thoughts that keep you from looking forward.

Your mind and heart have many wonderful things to
dwell on each day. Give thanks to God for placing a
rainbow of promise in your path.

*Dear God: Thank you for the wonderful and creative
work you are doing in my life. Help me look
forward to each new day. Amen.*

Forget the former things; do not dwell on the past.
See, I am doing a new thing!

ISAIAH **43:18–19** NIV

THE GOOD LIFE

Good people can look forward to a bright future.
PROVERBS 13:9 NCV

What makes for a good life? Laughter and happy times come to mind. You might also be thinking of those times you did the right thing without worrying about what the future would bring.

In those positive moments, God steps in with words of comfort and assurance. He praises us for following his commandments and gives us the strength to keep on going. Then he adds a promise. He tells us to look forward to tomorrow with hope and expectation. He says we can get excited about the future.

Rest in the peace of knowing you're doing the right thing. And smile, because the best is yet to come.

God in heaven: When things look hopeless to me,
help me look to you for my hope. In you
alone I put my trust. Amen.

*I know the thoughts that I think toward you, says
the L<small>ORD</small>, thoughts of peace and not of evil,
to give you a future and a hope.*

J<small>EREMIAH</small> 29:11 NKJV

SPIRITUAL SAVVY

*See that you go on growing in the Lord, and become
strong and vigorous in the truth you were taught.*

COLOSSIANS 2:7 TLB

To grow physically, the body needs the right kind of
food. The same can be said for spiritual growth.

God provides just the right spiritual diet through the wisdom
and promises of the Bible. He
spreads out a banquet in front of
you and says, "Come and eat of
my comfort, peace, and love.
Taste what I have to offer." When you do, your spirit
grows in knowledge and understanding. Your spirit gains
the strength, energy, and vitality God intends for you.

Accept God's invitation. Sit down to feast at his banquet
every day. It will keep your spirit growing and sustained.

*Thank you, God, for the spiritual nourishment of
the Bible and for all the ways I can exercise
my spirit in my daily life. Amen.*

*Like newborn babies, long for the pure milk
of the word, that by it you may grow.*

1 PETER 2:2 NASB

FACTS OF LIFE ETERNAL

*By his Spirit [God] has stamped us with his eternal
pledge—a sure beginning of what he is
destined to complete.*

2 CORINTHIANS 1:21–22 MSG

You have picked up this book and are reading these
words. Do you know what that says about you? It says
loudly and clearly that God's Spirit
is at work in you!

God's Spirit at work in you proves
two things: First, God has claimed
you as his own and you belong to
him. Second, God's claim means he
has plans for you. He plans to stay
close beside you today and every day
of your life, and he plans for you to live with him forever
in heaven.

You're a woman who belongs to God today, tomorrow,
and forever.

*Heavenly Father: Because I am yours, I can live today
with confidence and look forward to living
with you in heaven forever. Amen.*

Having believed, you were marked in him with a seal, the promised Holy Spirit.

EPHESIANS 1:13 NIV

GOOD CHOICES

I do not run without a goal. I fight like a boxer
who is hitting something—not just the air.
1 CORINTHIANS 9:26 NCV

Throughout history, dedicated women have worked to establish educational and social opportunities for girls and women. Their perseverance has opened a world of opportunity.

With opportunity comes the privilege and obligation to make wholesome, meaningful, and God-pleasing choices. You will know you have done so when you know the satisfaction of working toward an objective bigger than yourself and using your gifts unselfishly on those around you. Your ideals keep you moving toward that objective, persevering even when it's not personally convenient, keeping you focused on truth and goodness.

With God, your aim is lofty and you reach high because you have looked on high for your goals and ambitions.

Dear God: Thank you for the opportunities available to me. Guide me as I choose my life's goals and plans. Amen.

Run in such a way as to get the prize.

1 CORINTHIANS 9:24 NIV

GUIDANCE ON THE GO

Guide my steps by your word,
so I will not be overcome by evil.
PSALM 119:133 NLT

Female drivers are thought to be more willing than male drivers to ask directions when they're lost on the highway. Remember when you're feeling lost in life that God

offers guidance to let us know we are on the right path.

Sometimes the unanticipated happens. You might see several available courses of action but aren't sure which one to

choose. When you don't know which way to turn, never hesitate to ask God for directions. Let him point out the way he would have you go. Changes in your relationships, health, or situation can bring new challenges and opportunities. Asking God will help show you the way.

Dear God: So many times in my life I need
your wisdom and guidance. Thank you
for always being there for me. Amen.

The LORD will guide you continually,
And satisfy your soul in drought . . . .
You shall be like a watered garden.

ISAIAH 58:11 NKJV

TO YOUR HEALTH

*"I will restore health to you and heal you
of your wounds," says the* LORD.

JEREMIAH 30:17 NKJV

In recent times great strides have been made in women's medical care. Physicians are now aware more than ever

before of conditions and symptoms specific to women, and more treatment options have become available.

God has never needed to increase his attention to you. He has always been aware of, and provided, the care you need. Whenever you are ill or in pain, he is there with his healing touch. Whether your pain is of body, mind, or spirit, God will help you through it. If you're hurting right now, reach out to him for support. You are sure to feel his comfort and his peace.

*Great Healer: Bless the health-care providers for all they
do each day. Thank you for your healing touch that
surpasses all earthly resources. Amen.*

Beloved, I pray that all may go well with you
and that you may be in good health, just as
it is well with your soul.

3 JOHN 2 NRSV

THE OASIS

*Our lives get in step with God and all
others by letting him set the pace.*
ROMANS 3:27 MSG

If you're like most women, your calendar overflows with
things to do and places to go. Slowing down is very difficult in this fast-paced world.

Like a cool oasis, God offers a haven
from the pressure of activity and the
physical and spiritual fatigue it can
bring. He wants you to live life to the
fullest, so he opens his arms and welcomes your weary spirit. He says "slow
down" not to hold you back but to
refresh and restore you, leaving you confident in his love.

The most important thing on your busy calendar each
day is the time you spend in his embrace. With that, all
things are possible.

*Dear God: Thank you for giving me this time of
peace and contemplation. I need and desire
my time of rest in you. Amen.*

Oh, that my steps might be steady,
keeping to the course you set.

PSALM 119:5 MSG

POISED FOR ACTION

The LORD will be your confidence, and will keep your foot from being caught.

PROVERBS 3:26 NKJV

You can find any number of self-help books intended to bolster your confidence. In them, you may discover some useful ideas to improve your outlook, but the books  rarely mention where genuine self-assurance comes from.

Teresa of Avila said, "Let us remember that within us there is a palace of immense magnificence." God says he lives within each believing heart, and he lives in you. The immense magnificence of God's Spirit in you is the reason you can be sure of yourself in any situation. This is the true source of self-confidence. Knowing that God lives within you, and will never fail you, means that no obstacle is too great.

Dear God: I'm in awe as I contemplate your presence within me. Your Spirit gives me all the assurance I need to handle every circumstance that comes my way. Amen.

God has given us his Spirit. That is how we know that we are one with him, just as he is one with us.

1 JOHN 4:13 CEV

INSIDE OUT

Be content with what you have.

HEBREWS 13:5 NRSV

Perhaps you know a woman who simply radiates inner peace. In all likelihood, her contentment has nothing to do with how much money she has or her station in life.

These external things cannot bring true satisfaction. Soul-deep peace comes from the inside.

No matter what circumstances surround you in life right now, you can possess the priceless treasure called contentment. It starts with knowing yourself as a woman loved by God, and it blossoms as you fully accept his will for your life. Joyously embrace those blessings he gives and continues to give, and you will find that inner peace you want and deserve.

God of peace: I give myself and all I am to you.
Grant me the serenity of a heart and
mind at peace in you. Amen.

*The fear of the L\ORD leads to life: then one rests
content, untouched by trouble.*

PROVERBS 19:23 NIV

GIFT OF THE HEART

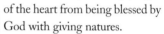

*Be kind and good to others; then you will
live safely here in the land and prosper.*

PSALM 37:3 TLB

Women often devote much of their lives to the happiness and well-being of others. To some, it is simply a gift

of the heart from being blessed by God with giving natures.

God speaks to you about the way he would have you respond to others, no matter what role or roles you play. It is his desire that all people work together in a spir-

it of love, compassion, and generosity. Mutual respect, shared affection, and reciprocal kindness lead to godly relationships. In some relationships, God invites you to take the first step. In each relationship, your giving nature is the key to doing God's will here on earth.

*Dear God: Thank you for all the relationships in my life.
Grant me the generosity of spirit to bless each
relationship with godly love. Amen.*

*Whoever has the gift of encouraging
others should encourage.*

ROMANS 12:8 NCV

GOOD EVIDENCE

The heavens keep telling the wonders of God,
and the skies declare what he has done.

PSALM 19:1 CEV

As you stand in awe of a sunset or are enthralled by a rainbow, you may find yourself contemplating God's magnif-

icent handiwork. Clearly, the beauty, brilliance, and mystery of the universe attest to God's presence and his power.

Because God has sent his Spirit to work in you, your life offers evidence of God's presence and power. You conform your thoughts, words, and actions to his will. Your very being announces his living and personal goodness. Those who look at you see what his Spirit has done. His glory shines brightly in you. God's strength becomes your strength.

Dear God: Grant me a heart of praise
for the wonders of your creation
and gratitude for the goodness you
have worked in me. Amen.

We rejoice in the hope of the glory of God.

ROMANS 5:2 NIV

Overcoming

LIGHTEN THE LOAD

Do not fear or be dismayed; tomorrow go out against them, for the LORD is with you.

2 CHRONICLES 20:17 NKJV

Imagine yourself weighed down with several heavy bags of groceries. Just as you realize they're too much for you to manage, a friend comes along to help you. What relief  when she lifts the load from your arms!

When the weight of worry and anxiety burdens your heart, God will be there beside you. With outstretched arms, he lifts your burdens and takes care of them for you. He knows what you're going through, and you can trust him with all the details, big and small. Tell him everything. He will give you the strength and wisdom you need to overcome the hardships you are facing.

God in heaven: Thank you for taking my burdens. With you beside me, I can emerge triumphant from any struggle. Amen.

Blessed be the Lord, who daily bears our burden.

PSALM 68:19 NASB

BOLD MOVE

*Do not fear, for I am with you, do not be afraid, for I
am your God; I will strengthen you, I will help you,
I will uphold you with my victorious right hand.*

ISAIAH 41:10 NRSV

When you were a little girl, you may have been afraid to
enter a darkened room or sleep without a night-light. In
our youthful imaginations, all sorts of
dangers lurked in the dark.

As adults, we know light dispels dark
shadows, and the best way to deal with
uncertainties is to shine a light into
dark places. Faith in God is the
lantern that banishes shadows and
lights the way to true happiness. Your faith in God's
unwavering presence gives you courage. If the dangers
are real, you can face them, with his help.

Walk with God, because he walks with you. You can rest
at ease in his light.

> *Heavenly Father: Thanks to you, I possess
> everything I need to face the future with
> boldness and strength. Amen.*

Fear not, O land; Be glad and rejoice,
For the LORD has done marvelous things!

JOEL 2:21 NKJV

GOD'S WAYS

Be merciful to those who doubt.

JUDE 22 NIV

In the Bible, Hannah was a woman who grieved because she was barren. She prayed deeply for a child; then, confident in God's willingness to answer, she returned to her daily life. In his own time, God granted her prayer.

Hannah's trust and patience brought her peace, even without proof that God would answer right away. In the same manner, questions of faith and belief often require God's own timing. Uncertainties you bring before him in prayer are addressed and resolved by God as you faithfully watch, wait, and learn of him.

With trust and patience, you will discover God's way in every circumstance and see doubt turned to faith.

Dear God: Guide me through the questions I have, and help me when I need understanding. Lead me to praise the glorious mystery of you. Amen.

Without wavering, let us hold tightly to the hope we say we have, for God can be trusted to keep his promise.

HEBREWS 10:23 NLT

GIVE GOD THE GLORY

Pride ends in a fall, while humility brings honor.
PROVERBS 29:23 TLB

When we are small, we are taught not to be arrogant.
Sometimes, however, we remember the lesson all too well
and cannot think of ourselves as gifted, valuable, and
worthy women.

Godly modesty is grounded in
the satisfaction of knowing
everything you are comes
from him. Consider your
progress on your spiritual
journey. Recognize God's
Spirit in you and contemplate his wondrous ways.
Where did all this come from?

Open yourself to the overwhelming joy of being his chosen instrument, and take great pleasure in the woman you
are. Then, give God all the credit and praise for what you
have become.

Dear God: Grant me a heart of true modesty and eyes to
recognize your continuing work in my life.
To you I give the glory! Amen.

The humble will inherit the land, and will delight themselves in abundant prosperity.

PSALM 37:11 NASB

A PEACEFUL PLACE

*It is hard to stop a quarrel once
it starts, so don't let it begin.*

PROVERBS 17:14 TLB

Like many women, you may feel irritable and perhaps
even angry. You are certainly not alone in your feelings.

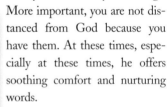

More important, you are not dis-
tanced from God because you
have them. At these times, especially at these times, he offers
soothing comfort and nurturing
words.

God encourages you to rest with
him in his unconditional love. Give him your worries,
stresses, aches, and pains. Talk to him about the annoy-
ances that seem to get under your skin at times, and let
him heal the wounds of your spirit. Open yourself to his
peace, and he will provide it just when you need it most.

*Dear God: In times when I feel my temper
flaring, let me run to the cool waters
of your calming presence. Amen.*

*The LORD is compassionate and gracious,
slow to anger, abounding in love.*

PSALM 103:8 NIV

RESTING IN HIM

*Jesus said: "Do not worry....Your heavenly Father
already knows all your needs."*
MATTHEW 6:31–32 NLT

During his earthly ministry, Jesus enjoyed visiting the
home of sisters Mary and Martha. One visit found
Martha so anxious about getting the meal ready she paid

scant attention to Jesus! The story
reminds us not to let concern over
petty details rob us of life's true
delights.

When you, like Martha's sister
Mary, sit at Jesus' feet and listen to
him, your priorities and responsibil-
ities fall into their proper place. Turn your eyes to the
God who gives you the skills, abilities, and resources you
require to effectively handle whatever situation arises in
your life. He knows what you need today, tomorrow, and
forever.

*Heavenly Father: Help me follow Mary's example,
and keep me secure in the knowledge that you
will take care of all my needs. Amen.*

*Do not worry about anything, but in everything by
prayer and supplication with thanksgiving let
your requests be made known to God.*

PHILIPPIANS 4:6 NRSV

REMEMBER TO RECYCLE

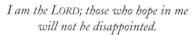

*I am the LORD; those who hope in me
will not be disappointed.*

ISAIAH 49:23 NIV

If you recycle, you've asked yourself this question: "How can I use this instead of throwing it away?" When life lets you down, you might imagine God asking you,

"Beloved woman, how can we turn this setback into something good and useful?"

When you turn your eyes to him, your setback will become experience and serve as a useful reminder to look forward in faith to the next opportunity he offers you. It will serve to keep you mindful of his providential care, and it prepares you to explore, discover, and pursue great things.

Use and reuse your experiences, and he will turn disappointments into victories.

*Dear God: You have excellent plans for me,
and I know all your plans will work out for
my good and well-being. Amen.*

None of those who wait for You will be ashamed.

PSALM 25:3 NASB

LIVING WATER

*The LORD will not cast off his people,
nor will he forsake his inheritance.*

PSALM 94:14 NKJV

The Bible tells of a woman who came to draw water
from the community well. For reasons of her own, she
chose to come when she would not encounter other

women. She didn't worry about
the lone man sitting nearby,
because he certainly would not
speak to her.

But he did speak. Though Jesus
knew all about her, he chose
instead to look into her heart, and
there he found a woman thirsting for true love, compassion, and acceptance.

Jesus came into the world to refresh you with God's
strength and assurance, and he welcomes you into his
presence. He accepts you just as you are, right to the
innermost yearnings of your heart.

> *Dear God: Thank you for welcoming me
> with open arms and accepting me just as
> I am in body, mind, and spirit. Amen.*

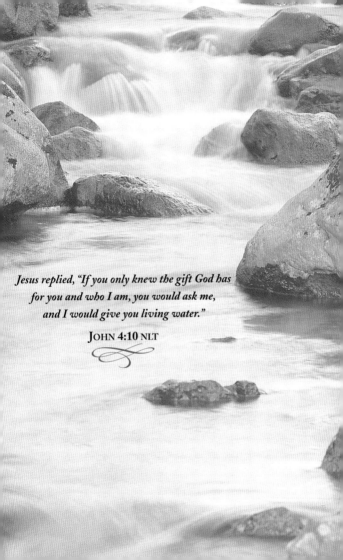

Jesus replied, "If you only knew the gift God has
for you and who I am, you would ask me,
and I would give you living water."

JOHN 4:10 NLT

LIGHT OF DAY

The LORD is near to the brokenhearted,
and saves the crushed in spirit.

PSALM 34:18 NRSV

We've all been down in the dumps. Maybe it's just one of those days, or maybe it's more serious than that, but you feel you're in the heart of a dark cloud.

 When you encounter one of those days, hold faithfully to prayer. Use prayer to lay out before God the whole of your sadness, even if you have trouble finding the right words. Wrap yourself in the certain knowledge that he hears you and will respond to you with care and concern, sensitivity and understanding. Be patient, even if you do not feel his presence. His light in your life will come as sure as the sun rises each day.

Dear God: Thank you for the knowledge
that you are always nearby even when
I'm unable to sense the precious gift
of your presence. Amen.

*I satisfy the weary ones and refresh
everyone who languishes.*

JEREMIAH 31:25 NASB

HEART OF PEACE

*Live in harmony by showing love for each
other. Be united in what you think,
as if you were only one person.*

In any relationship, a time comes when you and the
other person disagree. In the Bible, God offers a way to

handle the situation so your
relationship remains strong,
healthy, and vibrant.

It pleases God when you willingly promote harmony and
peace. Consider being the one
who chooses not to take offense

at the carelessly spoken remark, or being the first to
point out those things the two of you agree on and the
value of your relationship. Imagine the outcome if you
were always to care more about the other person than
about winning. Strive for peace, and see how all your
relationships strengthen, deepen, and endure.

*Heavenly Father: Put in me a peaceful heart,
and teach me to choose my words carefully
when I am in difficult situations. Amen.*

It's a mark of good character to avert quarrels.

PROVERBS 20:3 MSG

THE SEEDS OF WONDERS

*He said to me, "My grace is sufficient for you, for
My strength is made perfect in weakness."*
2 CORINTHIANS 12:9 NKJV

A woman, excited about her new property, planted a big
garden. Though books advise novices to start small, and
friends questioned the size of her project, she enthusias-

tically forged ahead with her
plans. Soon the care and main-
tenance of her lot overwhelmed
her. She admitted, "I've learned
a lesson—the hard way."

If you have learned a lesson
through an unfortunate experi-
ence, give thanks, because you are on the road to spiritual
maturity and wisdom. You have discovered the value of
good counsel and the merit of careful judgment. This is
knowledge you can take and use in every future endeavor.

In the seeds of frailty, God plants mighty wonders.

*Dear God: Thank you for supporting me and
strengthening me so I can become the woman
you have created me to be. Amen.*

We know that in all things God works for the good of those who love him, who have been called according to his purpose.

ROMANS 8:28 NIV

SPA TIME

*Those who let distress drive them away
from God are full of regrets.*

2 CORINTHIANS 7:10 MSG

For many, there's nothing more soothing than soaking in a deep, warm bubble bath. Minor aches and pains seem to drift away, you are refreshed and rejuvenated, and the

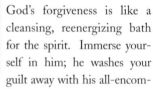

moments of quiet ease the mind as well.

God's forgiveness is like a cleansing, reenergizing bath for the spirit. Immerse yourself in him; he washes your guilt away with his all-encompassing comfort and the assurance of his love. You are given the healing balm of complete pardon, and you emerge ready and able to follow him more closely and listen to him more attentively.

God's way changes you, and always for the better.

*Dear God: Thank you for replacing my sadness and guilt
with joy and thanksgiving. Bathe me in the
refreshing waters of your peace. Amen.*

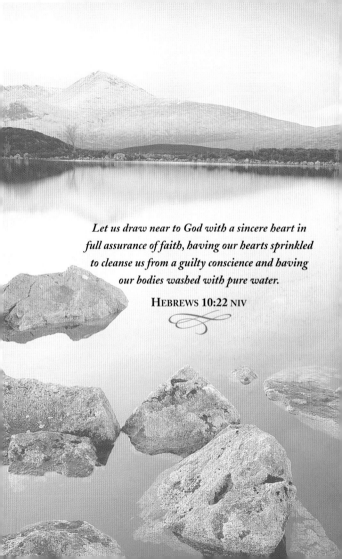

Let us draw near to God with a sincere heart in full assurance of faith, having our hearts sprinkled to cleanse us from a guilty conscience and having our bodies washed with pure water.

HEBREWS 10:22 NIV

IN HIS PRESENCE

I am continually with you; you hold my right hand.

PSALM 73:23 NRSV

You can feel lonely in a room by yourself, and you can feel lonely in a crowd. You may not understand why you are overcome with the sense of distance and separation  that can make you feel small and weak. Whatever the cause, God offers a guaranteed solution.

Meditate on God's love for you, a love beyond all human understanding. Because he values you so much, he has promised to never let you move out of his embrace or away from his hand of goodness. By yourself or in a crowd, you can rely on God, who is always by your side. With God, you are never alone.

God in heaven: I give thanks to you for the security
of knowing you are with me wherever I go.
I am never alone. Amen.

God is...right there with you. He won't let you down; he won't leave you.

DEUTERONOMY 31:6 MSG

TRUE FREEDOM

*God can be trusted not to let you be tempted
too much, and he will show you how to
escape from your temptations.*

1 CORINTHIANS 10:13 CEV

As you understand more about God's love for you, you
may find yourself becoming more aware of temptations

in your life that do not fit in with
his purpose for you.

It pleases God when you tell him
about the appeal these things may
have for you. He cares and understands and will help you overcome
their allure. You will walk away

from them stronger than before. Your urges and earthly
desires do not possess the kind of power God has, and he
promises to give his power to you. God created you to be
free, and he doesn't want you to give that freedom away
to anyone or anything.

*Dear God: Remove the barriers in front of me.
I need your strength and power to keep on your
path of peace, goodness, and joy. Amen.*

Be strong in the Lord and
in his mighty power.

EPHESIANS 6:10 NLT

Discovering

ETERNAL PLEDGE

All the promises of God in Him are Yes, and in Him
Amen, to the glory of God through us.
2 CORINTHIANS 1:20 NKJV

"I promise." The intent of those words, when uttered this side of heaven, sometimes falls short. When uttered by God, those two words point to an unbreakable and unchanging pledge you can rely on.

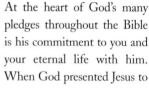

At the heart of God's many pledges throughout the Bible is his commitment to you and your eternal life with him. When God presented Jesus to take your place on the cross, he confirmed his vow to offer salvation to you and all people. His Spirit's work in your life right now shows God cares for you and waits for you to accept the many marvelous promises he has made.

Heavenly Father: Your promises amaze and humble
me. It is my privilege and pleasure to receive your
magnificent gifts. Amen.

The LORD is faithful in all his words,
and gracious in all his deeds.

PSALM 145:13 NRSV

FREE FOR THE TAKING

*How rich is God's grace, which he has
given to us so fully and freely.*
EPHESIANS 1:7–8 NCV

Whether you were born-to-shop or are someone who
goes shopping only out of necessity, you know you never
get something of value for nothing. If someone offers you

an expensive item at no cost, you have
every reason to start asking questions.

The rules of the earthly marketplace
don't apply in heaven. God's compassion
comes to you completely free. You need
only accept it. He guarantees you his
mercy and kindness now and throughout
eternity. It's simply God's good pleasure to show such
love to you.

Put away your wallet and open yourself to the wonder of
God's grace. It's yours for the taking.

*Dear God: I give thanks for the mercy, compassion,
and kindness you show toward me. You
have been gracious to me. Amen.*

*From his abundance we have all received
one gracious blessing after another.*

JOHN 1:16 NLT

BOUNTIFUL AND BEAUTIFUL

*Jesus said: "The thief comes only to steal and kill
and destroy; I came that they may have life,
and have it abundantly."*
JOHN 10:10 NASB

Think of the woman you most admire. Chances are she
inspires you to strive for excellence and motivates you to

make changes for the better in
your life. Simply put, her example leads you to enrich your life.

In the same way, God wants to
enrich your life with his many
and plentiful blessings. When
you look up to him, you see the beauty and peace he
offers, and you begin to bring those things into your life.
As you read the Bible, you learn more about God, and
you find yourself making choices and decisions based on
his will.

For a bountiful and beautiful life, look up to him.

*Dear God: Thank you for showing me how full, rich,
and abundant life can be. I cherish the blessings
you show me each day. Amen.*

Return, O my soul, to your rest, for the LORD
has dealt bountifully with you.

PSALM **116:7** NRSV

OUT OF THE BLUE

*We'll never comprehend all the great things he does;
his miracle-surprises can't be counted.*
JOB 9:10 MSG

You've heard the expression "Life is full of surprises," and you probably can think of several examples from your own experience. When you couldn't see a solution to a problem, one popped up seemingly out of nowhere.

God moves events to work for your good, even when you don't understand why something is happening to you. He cares about your plans for the day, week, and year, but he sees your plans in light of all eternity, and he may choose to provide for you in a way you could not have anticipated.

When you walk with God, expect the unexpected. He has great and joyful things waiting for you.

*Dear God: In difficult days when I have no
answers, grant me patience as I await
the joyful news you have in
store for me. Amen.*

May the Lord direct your hearts to the love of God
and to the steadfastness of Christ.

2 THESSALONIANS 3:5 NRSV

HEAVENLY JOY

God's kingdom...[is] what God does with your
life as he sets it right, puts it together,
and completes it with joy.
ROMANS 14:17 MSG

As a little child, you may have pictured heaven as a far-
away place with beautiful angels floating around castles

that glittered in the sun. You
were correct in thinking that
heaven is a realm of breathtaking
beauty, but through God's Spirit,
it isn't so very far away.

God brings the beauty of heaven
to you as his Spirit works peace,
joy, loveliness, and goodness in your heart. Day by day,
your God-pleasing thoughts, words, and actions increas-
ingly transform you into a woman of transcendent beauty, a woman in whom God's Spirit lives and breathes, a
woman who enjoys the sweet closeness of heaven right
here on Earth.

Heavenly Father: Open my heart to the
work of your Spirit in me, and allow me
to live each day in your love. Amen.

God's kingdom is within you.

LUKE **17:21** NCV

ALL GOOD THINGS

*See if I will not open the windows of heaven for
you and pour down for you an overflowing blessing.*
MALACHI 3:10 NRSV

You may have heard the saying "All things in modera-
tion." While it is good advice for our own conduct, it
isn't God's way of doing things. With his many and var-
ied blessings, he's downright extravagant.

God has provided a world of sunshine
and starshine, fields and seas, rivers and
mountains. He has blessed you with life
and breath, with thoughts, abilities, and a
heart turned toward knowing and loving
him. Thank him, and he says, "My
Beloved, you haven't seen anything yet. There is so much
more!"

There's no end to what God can and wants to do. With
all good things, God is a God of abundance.

*Dear God: Thank you for the good things you
have put into my life today. Keep me eternally
thankful for everything I receive. Amen.*

*May his blessings and peace be yours, sent to you
from God our Father and Jesus Christ our Lord.*

EPHESIANS 1:2 TLB

A HELPING HAND

Jesus said, "Here is a simple, rule-of-thumb guide for behavior: Ask yourself what you want people to do for you, then grab the initiative and do it for them."
MATTHEW 7:12 MSG

In your sincere desire to help others, do you sometimes find yourself wondering if getting involved would violate

a friend's privacy or undermine a neighbor's right to make her own decisions? It can be unsettling.

Jesus offers his perspective when he invites you to take a few moments to imagine yourself in the place of the other person. After reflecting on her fears, struggles, abilities, and resources, consider what you would most appreciate someone doing for you. Then confidently do the same thing for her.

Sometimes your act will be the perfect response and sometimes it won't, but every time you will be passing along the message that God cares.

Dear God: Grant me a heart of wisdom so I may reach out to others in genuinely helpful and caring ways. Amen.

Because of [Christ] all the parts of the body care for each other and help each other.

COLOSSIANS 2:19 ICB

FIRST PLACE

*Seek the Kingdom of God above all else, and live right-
eously, and he will give you everything you need.*
MATTHEW 6:33 NLT

Many women say they cherish the time they spend in
prayer during the quiet hours of the early morning. In
a truly physical way, they're giving God first place in
their day.

Getting up before dawn may not work
for you, but putting God first in your
thoughts, words, and actions yields
extraordinary rewards. You move with
God-given purpose, and you gain
peace of mind knowing you're doing
the right thing for the right reasons. Among the options
available to you, choose those things poised to enrich
your life and the lives of those around you.

All times of day (or night), let God come first in your life.

*Dear God: Grant me the willingness and
the courage to give you first place in my
thoughts, words, and actions. Amen.*

*Seek those things which
are above, where Christ
is, sitting at the right
hand of God.*

COLOSSIANS 3:1 NKJV

GOD'S ANSWER

Call to Me, and I will answer you,
and show you great and mighty things,
which you do not know.
JEREMIAH 33:3 NKJV

Are you a woman who is open to new ideas—someone
who longs to discover new things about God and his

ways? That kind of willingness to
learn pleases God, and he urges us
to explore even further by speaking
to him in prayer.

When you spend time in prayer,
you take advantage of the extraordinary privilege of placing your con-
cerns, hopes, anxieties, and plans in God's hands. True to
his promise, he takes them up as quickly as you release
them, and he assures you he cares and understands. Then
he says to you, "I know how all this will turn out. Watch
and listen, while I show you."

Heavenly Father: Thank you for the gift of
prayer and its power to change the
way I think, act, and feel. Amen.

The Lord . . . delights in the prayers of his people.

PROVERBS 15:8 TLB

COMPLIMENTS DUE

God takes particular pleasure in acts of worship—a different kind of "sacrifice"—that takes place in kitchen and workplace and on the streets.
HEBREWS 13:16 MSG

Studies have shown how receiving deserved compliments increases self-confidence and enhances self-esteem. Studies rarely mention, however, the benefits accrued by the person offering praise.

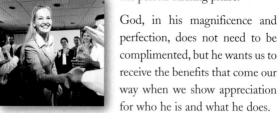

God, in his magnificence and perfection, does not need to be complimented, but he wants us to receive the benefits that come our way when we show appreciation for who he is and what he does.

When you acknowledge his greatness, you heighten your awareness of your humanity and your need for his help and strength. You also strengthen your faith by acknowledging that God is good and great and powerful enough to come to your aid. Give praise and open your heart to be blessed.

Dear God: Thank you for revealing yourself to me, and thank you for inviting me to join the heavens in worshiping you. Amen.

I will be glad and exult in you; I will sing praise to your name, O Most High.

PSALM 9:2 NRSV

HEIRLOOMS

*God has made everything beautiful
for its own time.*
ECCLESIASTES 3:11 NLT

Long ago, women's hands carefully crafted each block of a quilt. Each intricate shape made a perfect fit with the next, each section stitched together to create a breathtak-

ing work of art. As a cherished family heirloom, the quilts displayed the skill, creativity, and love of those women who went before.

The expanse of the sky, the songs of the streams, the scent of a blossom testify to God's creative mind and living power. You are heir to a world full of magnificent reminders of who God is and what he can do. He encourages you to admire his creation, treasure it, and contemplate his continuing love for you.

Father in heaven: Thank you for the magnificence of the universe and the tender beauties of nature. I cherish the inheritance you have given me. Amen.

God looked over all that he had made,
and it was excellent in every way.

GENESIS 1:31 TLB

LIFE'S PURPOSE

*Lead a life worthy of the calling to
which you have been called.*
EPHESIANS 4:1 NRSV

From early childhood, some girls know what they want
to do in life, and when they grow up, they do it. But most

of us need time to discover our
life's work, and we might even
take several detours before we
find our way.

God created you with a specific
purpose in mind, and he has
endowed you with all the gifts, talents, resources, and
opportunities you need to live out his plan for your life.
If the course ahead appears unclear to you, rest easy.
When you place your trust in his wisdom and in his love,
you're pointed in the right direction. You will find what
you seek.

*Heavenly Father: At every stage in my life,
direct me and guide me according to your
good and gracious will. Amen.*

We are His workmanship,
created in Christ Jesus for
good works, which God
prepared beforehand that
we should walk in them.

EPHESIANS 2:10 NKJV

YOUR CREATIVE LIGHT

*God created human beings in his image. In the
image of God he created them.*
GENESIS 1:27 NCV

A potter uses her hands to sculpt a bowl of extraordinary
beauty. A dancer enthralls the audience with expressive
movements. A poet touches hearts with evocative phrases.

 All these are expressions of cre-
ativity. But if you really want to see
a dazzling display of creativity,
consider this:

In you, God has fashioned a
home for his Spirit, and through
the presence of his Spirit, your
voice, hands, and feet express your unique ways of worshiping him. Through thoughtful words and compassionate actions, you mold relationships. Through the
careful attention you bring to even the smallest of tasks,
you evoke an aura of loveliness and peace. In God, your
creativity shines.

*Creator-God: Keep my heart and mind full of
thoughts, ideas, and dreams that flow into
creative expressions of love. Amen.*

I worship in adoration—what a creation!

PSALM 139:14 MSG

GOOD WORK

Enjoy the work you do here on earth.
Whatever work you do, do your best.
ECCLESIASTES 9:9–10 NCV

A routine transaction with a woman occupying a low-paying position leaves you uplifted and inspired. Why? Because she performed her job with dignity, grace, and

generosity of spirit, and she obviously cared about her work. You think, "If she can find satisfaction in her work, why can't I in mine?"

Similar incidents happen in all walks of life, and each shows how attitude more than circumstance determines how you feel about yourself and your work. Your willingness to do your best at whatever the day brings and seek the good in whatever situation you find yourself identifies you as a joyful woman of noble and godly character.

Dear God: Grant me a spirit of joy in
doing the work that lies before me each day.
In you I find my inspiration. Amen.

All to whom God gives wealth and possessions and whom he enables to enjoy them, and to accept their lot and find enjoyment in their toil—this is the gift of God.

ECCLESIASTES 5:19 NRSV

Developing

MAKING DISCIPLES

No discipline is enjoyable while it is happening—it is painful! But afterward there will be a peaceful harvest of right living for those who are trained in this way.
HEBREWS 12:11 NLT

The mother who disciplines her children in a loving and consistent manner earns their heartfelt respect and grat-

itude. They learn she cares about them enough to guide and instruct them as they grow.

God cares so much about you that he makes it known when you are veering away from his will for your life. He corrects you for the purpose of bringing you back and strengthening you, of teaching and training you. When you receive God's instruction, gladly accept it and learn from it, because his voice of authority is a sure indication that he sees you as one of his own precious children.

Heavenly Father: Thank you for the times you have corrected me and brought me back to you. I want to learn to grow and walk in discipleship. Amen.

My child, don't make light of the LORD's discipline, and don't give up when he corrects you. For the LORD disciplines those he loves.

HEBREWS 12:5–6 NLT

TO THE FINISH

*When your endurance is fully developed, you will
be perfect and complete, needing nothing.*
JAMES 1:4 NLT

Because she wanted to enter a marathon, a woman spent
several months in training. Each day she ran a little far-
ther until she could run the full distance, and on race day

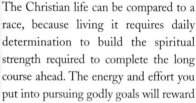

she ran the race to the finish.

The Christian life can be compared to a
race, because living it requires daily
determination to build the spiritual
strength required to complete the long
course ahead. The energy and effort you
put into pursuing godly goals will reward

you with the gifts of determination, fortitude, and satisfaction.

When challenges come, remember: God has promised to
see you through to the finish, but you must be prepared.

*O God: Create in me a spirit of determination, strength,
and stamina so I may remain surely and steadily on your
path. I want to run to the finish. Amen.*

Let us run with endurance the race
God has set before us.

HEBREWS **12:1** NLT

THE RIGHT THING

Wait on the LORD; be of good courage,
and He shall strengthen your heart.
PSALM 27:14 NKJV

We owe our gratitude to the untold numbers of women who have stood up for justice and truth. Because their voices were heard, laws changed, attitudes shifted, and

 educational and workplace opportunities opened and expanded for the generations that followed them.

In your own life, you demonstrate that same great courage when you choose what you know is right despite the difficulty, unpopularity, or likely consequences of your choice. Your own strength may falter when hardships come, and you may wonder if it's worth the struggle. God says "Yes, it is," and he will supply the courage you need if you rely on him when the time comes.

Dear God: Grant me the strength of heart and the
courage to do the right thing. I need your help to
stand firm against all opposition. Amen.

The Lord said: "Be strong and very courageous."

JOSHUA 1:7 NASB

WONDER WOMAN

Let the weak say, "I am strong."
JOEL 3:10 NKJV

Perhaps you know about Wonder Woman, the all-powerful comic book heroine, or maybe you remember the 1970s TV show based on her character. While the fictional fantasy entertains, God's power, strength, and wondrous acts are for real.

The spiritual strength you possess through God's Spirit gives you the ability to turn away from the crowd when it's going in the wrong direction. In life's troubles and times of hardship, God's stable, steady hand will see you through and bring about positive and productive ends.

In him, think of yourself as a woman with wondrous powers, and use your strength to achieve great things.

Dear God: As I learn more about you, I stand in
awe of your power. Grant me reliance on
you, source of all true strength, when I
face the trials and tests of life. Amen.

O LORD, be gracious to us; we long for you. Be our strength every morning, our salvation in time of distress.

ISAIAH 33:2 NIV

YES!

Let us be self-controlled, putting on faith and love as a breastplate, and the hope of salvation as a helmet.
1 THESSALONIANS 5:8 NIV

Some women claim the freedom to act as they choose. They seem to be having the time of their lives. You ask yourself why God tells you no in regard to certain behavior.

God's rules assist you in making life-affirming choices. He knows the world offers many attractive options, but not all of them are positive. While you can see the negative consequences of some, you cannot see far enough ahead to know the outcome of others. God sees, even to eternity, and he guides you toward those paths that will render a happy and prosperous future.

Rest assured, his "no" is your "yes" to a full, free, and joyful life.

Dear God: Thank you for guiding me in the right paths, and keep me faithful when I face a choice between self-gratification and self-control. Amen.

Prepare your minds for action; be self-controlled; set your hope fully on the grace to be given you when Jesus Christ is revealed.

1 PETER 1:13 NIV

WHAT THEY'RE SAYING

The integrity of the upright will guide them.
PROVERBS 11:3 NKJV

Dorcas was a member of the New Testament church. Known for her godly actions, consistent with her belief in Jesus, her life uplifted and encouraged believers, and her character brought many others into the early Christian church.

Your godly reputation depends on character, the unwavering connection between what you believe and what you do, and between unseen matters of the spirit and observable conduct with family, friends, associates, and even strangers. Your words, choices, attitude, and lifestyle show God's will and purpose for your life, and people will recognize you as a woman of honor and goodness. Wherever you go, your reputation is a credit to you—and God.

Dear God: Guide my ways so my words and actions testify to your goodness and a godly reputation reflects your work in my life. Amen.

Keep your eyes focused on what is right, and
look straight ahead to what is good.

PROVERBS 4:25 NCV

BOLD MOVE

The righteous are as bold as a lion.
PROVERBS 28:1 NRSV

Our culture generally ascribes valor to men. God, however, not only recognizes valor in women but insists that we demonstrate it.

Godly valor doesn't require you to growl like a lion, but to walk with the assurance of one confident in God's presence and power to make things work for you when you follow his lead. Your godly valor consists of the willingness to encourage goodness and purity in all matters, to remind others of God's all-encompassing love and universal truths, and to stand firm when someone snarls at you to back down from the righteous path.

Valor ranks as a trait highly becoming of you, a woman of God.

Heavenly Father: Help me grow in boldness so I will be
willing and able to act with godly valor in the
face of fear and temptation. Amen.

*When I called, you answered me; you
made me bold and stouthearted.*

PSALM 138:3 NIV

STRONG WORDS

*Deep in your hearts you know that every promise
of the LORD your God has come true.
Not a single one has failed!*
JOSHUA 23:14 NLT

"You have my word on it." In big matters as in small, the phrase signals an intention to follow through on a promise given, an objective stated.

Being true to your word is a God-pleasing and Godlike attribute. It's God-pleasing because constancy builds trust between you and others and enhances your reputation as a woman who does what she says she will do. It's Godlike because God is true to his Word, and in his Word he has declared to you his eternal love. Even if you falter in your promises, God remains unwavering in his promise to care for you. You have his Word on it.

*Dear God: Your infinite and steadfast fidelity
fills my heart with gratitude. Keep me firm
in my faithfulness to the promises
I make to others. Amen.*

Never let go of loyalty and faithfulness.

PROVERBS 3:3 GNT

IT'S CATCHING

God will yet fill your mouth with laughter.
JOB 8:21 NASB

Perhaps you have a friend whose effervescent laughter and joy lifts your heart. You can't help but share her joy in life.

A merry heart comes naturally as you grow closer to God and nurture your relationship with him. Refreshed by his words of hope, his promises, you become more open to the bright and playful aspects of life. You more fully appreciate the simple blessings surrounding you, and find heartfelt happiness in knowing all things rest in his hands. From there, your joy spreads to those around you.

Fill your heart with God's promises and let him show you the delightful side of his creation. His joy is contagious!

Dear God: Grant me the ability to see and appreciate the humor in life and share the gift of a merry heart with those in need of laughter and joy. Amen.

A merry heart makes a cheerful countenance.

PROVERBS 15:13 NKJV

GOOD CHEER

Be made new in the attitude of your minds.
EPHESIANS 4:23 NIV

Martha Washington once said, "I've learned from experience that the greater part of our happiness or misery depends on our dispositions and not on our circumstances."

When you commit yourself to optimism, adverse circumstances shrink to their proper size. Your positive outlook enables you to see the best and make the best of situations. Good things begin to happen because of your constructive and purposeful thinking, words, and actions. You learn you can cope, and cope well, and you find great and lasting pleasure in your God-given strengths and abilities.

A cheerful disposition looks at the world through the eyes of God's life-affirming goodness and love.

Dear God: Renew in me a godly attitude of optimism, and restore my mind with confidence in your willingness to see me through whatever comes my way in life. Amen.

*Your attitude should
be the kind that
was shown us by
Jesus Christ.*

PHILIPPIANS 2:5 TLB

RIGHT AND WRONG

*Therefore I do my best always to have a clear
conscience toward God and all people.*
ACTS 24:16 NRSV

Many women avoid drawing a clear distinction between
right and wrong for fear of appearing intolerant. They
often find, however, their consciences are then clouded
by doubt.

The Bible offers God's clear perspective. First, he wants you to know the difference between right and wrong, so he sets out his commandments and his will for your relationships and your actions. Second, he wants you to possess a conscience free of misgivings. He graces you with cleansing forgiveness and renewing strength so you can distinguish right from wrong freely and without reservation. Third, he invites you deeper into the Bible to discover more about his unchanging truth, wisdom, and holiness.

*Dear God: Bathe my conscience in the wisdom of your
Word and strengthen my resolve to live your principles
of truth and justice. Amen.*

This command is love, which comes from a pure heart and a good conscience and a sincere faith.

1 TIMOTHY 1:5 NIV

EXPECT THE BEST

*My soul, wait silently for God alone,
for my expectation is from Him.*
PSALM 62:5 NKJV

Many women anticipate great things, while other women anticipate great things and set about to make them happen. Which applies to you?

Your dream about the future and all the good things it may hold for you pleases God, yet he asks you to do more than simply sit and expect a positive outcome. He delights to see you involved in working toward your great tomorrow by doing today whatever supports your purpose and brings your hopes and dreams to fruition. All the while, God supports you by assuring you of his excellent plans for you, his constant presence, and his unconditional love.

*Heavenly Father: Hold me in your
strong arms as I put my godly
expectations into practice in
productive and purposeful
ways. Amen.*

*The eyes of all look expectantly to You. . . . You open
Your hand and satisfy the desire of every living thing.*

PSALM 145:15–16 NKJV

FARSIGHTED

*"My thoughts are not your thoughts, neither are
your ways my ways," declares the LORD.*
ISAIAH 55:8 NIV

Now that you're an adult, you see things differently than
when you were a little girl. You possess a perspective
unavailable to you before, a perspective that continues to
broaden and deepen as you
embrace more of life. Even if
you live to a grand old age, however, you will never gain God's
vast perspective.

Consider where God has
been—before time began, when he created the world.
Throughout history he was there. Meditate on what he
sees—before you were born, he saw you and each day of
your life. No wonder his ways seem mysterious! God's
perspective includes earth and heaven and eternity.

*O God: When I don't understand, keep me
mindful of your infinite wisdom; and when
I don't see, help me remember your
eternal point of view. Amen.*

Let God transform you into a new person by changing the way you think.

ROMANS 12:2 NLT

A BIBLICAL MIND

*God wants the combination of his steady, constant
calling and warm, personal counsel in Scripture to
come to characterize us.*
ROMANS 15:4 MSG

God promises to keep you mindful of his words, but for
him to remind you, you need to know what he has said.

For this reason, your continued
growth and maturity as a Christian
comes with a practical and practicable Bible study plan.

How long you spend in God's Word
depends on what you're able to
accomplish. Five minutes of attentive
reading achieves more than an hour
of study planned but never spent. You can find Bible
study aids in bookstores and online, along with com-
mentaries to explain meaning and context. Also, group
Bible study works to keep you committed and account-
able, and also offers the gift of Christian fellowship.

*Dear God: Teach me to know and love you through
your Word, and grant me the godly commitment
I need to learn from you. Amen.*

Jesus said to them . . . "Others, like seed sown on good soil, hear the word, accept it, and produce a crop—thirty, sixty or even a hundred times what was sown."

MARK 4:13, 20 NIV

Learning

AT HOME

Jesus said: "Look at me. I stand at the door. I knock. If you hear me call and open the door, I'll come right in and sit down to supper with you."
REVELATION 3:20 MSG

Think of a place where you feel most at home. Perhaps it's a cozy corner of a favorite room, or a spot outside

where you savor the view and the sounds of nature. Now you have a sense of God's feelings as he finds a place in your heart.

Like the most gracious of guests, God enters in peace and goodwill and puts himself at your service. He listens as you speak, cares about

what you're going through, and offers his support, encouragement, and partnership. As your faith opens your heart to him, he opens his strength and wisdom to you.

Your divine guest feels right at home in you.

Dear God: Thank you for entering my life with your divine presence. Keep me ever mindful of you, my heart's most honored guest. Amen.

Jesus said, "Indeed, the kingdom of God is within you."

LUKE 17:21 NKJV

WHY?

*We have not stopped praying for you and asking
God to fill you with the knowledge of his will
through all spiritual wisdom and understanding.*
COLOSSIANS 1:9 NIV

If you have been in a tragic situation, you know what it's
like to ask God "why." God hears and uses your "why" to
strengthen you and bring you his
peace.

When you cry out to him, you are
naming the burden of your heart and
presenting him with the fullness of
your emotions. Your straightforward
prayer shows you are facing your fears
and opening yourself to spiritual growth, insight, and maturity. As you meditate on his Word and listen for his answer,
you discern where God would have you go from here.

Peace, founded on full surrender to God's purpose, is his
compassionate answer to your cry of "why."

*Heavenly Father: When I don't understand and
my strength fails, grant me readiness to rely
solely on your will and find peace in
surrendering to your wisdom. Amen.*

I trust in you, O Lᴏʀᴅ; I say, "You are my God."
My times are in your hand.

Pꜱᴀʟᴍ 31:14–15 ɴʀꜱᴠ

LEAN ON HIM

Trust in the Lord with all your heart. Do not depend on your own understanding.
PROVERBS 3:5 NIrV

While the "independent woman" stands as an icon to self-sufficiency and personal savvy, her liberty is limited unless she humbly confesses her reliance on God.

God has blessed you with certain skills, resources, and opportunities, and he is pleased when you use these things to their fullest potential. As you do, you will find he entrusts you with even more marvelous gifts, and these, too, he has given you for your good and the benefit of others.

With your efforts, you develop into a woman who knows her own mind and handles her responsibilities well, a truly independent woman. It happens when you place your reliance on God.

Dear God: I depend on you for the genuine independence of heart and mind I need to trust in you and learn your wondrous ways. Amen.

You, LORD, give true peace to those who depend on you, because they trust you.

ISAIAH 26:3 NCV

RIGHT LIVING

*Jesus came to them and said, "Go and make disciples
of all nations . . . teaching them to obey
everything I have commanded you."*
MATTHEW 28:18–20 NIV

Though God's rules may never win a popularity contest,
he has given them for pure and noble purposes to those
who are willing to listen.

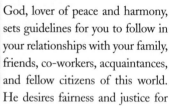

God, lover of peace and harmony,
sets guidelines for you to follow in
your relationships with your family,
friends, co-workers, acquaintances,
and fellow citizens of this world.
He desires fairness and justice for
all, and he shows you how to achieve those ends, even
when doing so might prove inconvenient for you.

God, lover of the highest good, implores you to put his
commandments into practice, because when you do, all
his gifts, benefits, and blessings fill your life.

*Dear God: Put in me a willing and obedient spirit,
and grant me the wisdom to listen to your
teachings and apply your commandments to
my thoughts, words, and actions. Amen.*

Happy are those who fear the LORD, who greatly delight in his commandments.

PSALM 112:1 NRSV

GOD'S GOOD TIME

Restore to me the joy of your salvation,
and sustain in me a willing spirit.
PSALM 51:12 NRSV

We're accustomed to getting things done in a hurry, and
we purchase gadgets and appliances promising speed and

convenience. As we learn more about
God, however, we realize he keeps a
different pace, moving in his own time
and according to his highest purposes.

When you willingly wait on God for
the desires of your heart, you expand
and deepen your worship of him to
include godly patience and trust. In
your willing submission to his pace, you prove you truly
have confidence in his wisdom and his timetable. Your
peace of mind leaves you free to truly enjoy the moment,
knowing and believing time belongs to God.

Heavenly Father: When I come before you with the
desires of my heart, grant me the will to wait on you in
quiet expectation and with godly hope. Amen.

The Lord is good to those who wait for him, to the soul that seeks him.

LAMENTATIONS 3:25 NRSV

ATTENTION, PLEASE

Keep your guard up....
Keep a firm grip on the faith.
1 Peter 5:9 MSG

Imagine you're supervising a child who asks if she can walk to a friend's house several blocks away. You give your permission, but first you remind her of the traffic

and warn her to pay close attention as she crosses a busy intersection.

In the Bible, God identifies sin so you will be fully aware of its dangers and the consequences of wrongdoing. Then he promises you his strength as you hold on to his words and rely on his warnings, applying his guidance and direction as you go forward with your life. Remain vigilant, he says, because vigilance will keep you safe from harm.

Heavenly Father: Grant me an attentive
heart and a vigilant spirit so I will
hear and heed your warnings
offered to me in love. Amen.

Be very careful, then, how you live—
not as unwise but as wise.

EPHESIANS 5:15 NIV

A TEACHABLE MOMENT

We should make plans—
counting on God to direct us.
PROVERBS 16:9 TLB

You know the feeling—you had everything planned, then something happened along the way to turn your plans inside out. You could think of these times as God's teachable moments.

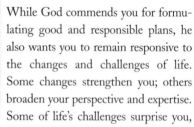

While God commends you for formulating good and responsible plans, he also wants you to remain responsive to the changes and challenges of life. Some changes strengthen you; others broaden your perspective and expertise. Some of life's challenges surprise you, startle you, amaze you, or even mystify you. All, however, come to you as opportunities from God to walk ever more closely with him.

Let the next "teachable moment" find you open to God's good plans for you.

Heavenly Father: In your love, grant me the willingness to adapt my plan to your plans, my time to your purposes, my desires to your will. Amen.

My times are in Your hand.

PSALM 31:15 NKJV

MARK YOUR WORDS

Those who speak with care will be rewarded.
PROVERBS 18:21 NCV

From early childhood, we begin to understand the power of words. We learn how words can please others, make friends, solve problems, and comfort hurting hearts. In the Bible, God calls to mind these truths.

The words you use reflect your attitude and feelings toward others, and well-chosen, timely words show your positive engagement with the world around you. When you express yourself for the purpose of building up people, contributing to the common well-being, and advancing worthy causes, your communication advances God's work in the world.

Even when you aren't talking about God, your godly words reflect your discipleship and prove an effective witness to his work in your life.

Dear God: When I communicate with others, help me choose words with care and compassion so they reflect your gracious words of love to me. Amen.

*To make an apt answer is a joy to anyone,
and a word in season, how good it is!*

PROVERBS 15:23 NRSV

UNLIMITED POSSIBILITIES

*It is required that those who have been
given a trust must prove faithful.*
1 CORINTHIANS 4:2 NIV

God never asks for the impossible, but he often makes
the impossible happen when someone uses the abilities
and resources he has provided.

 You possess everything you
need to perform what God
requires of you this day, and for
that reason, how you use his
gifts matters to him. He insists
on accountability. He knows
that your mindful assessment of
your gifts and how you use them will do two things.
First, it compels your gratitude to God for all he has
given to you; and second, it encourages you to identify
and develop your gifts to the fullest.

See what's possible when you use what he has provided.

*Dear God: Thank you for the abilities and resources you
have seen fit to give me. Keep me committed to their
continual development and constant use. Amen.*

Good stewards of the manifold grace of God,
serve one another with whatever gift
each of you has received.

1 PETER 4:10 NRSV

TRANQUIL WATERS

*O Lord, you will ordain peace for us, for indeed, all
that we have done, you have done for us.*
ISAIAH 26:12 NRSV

If you're like most women, you fill many roles. Pressure
can arise when these roles conflict, and sometimes it can

be overwhelming and plunge you into
a sea of stress. God understands the
agony of stress, and he provides relief
for its presence in your life.

God says, "Bring your troubles to me
and leave them with me." He knows
the burden you're carrying can be too
heavy and hard for you to bear. Once
you let him lift the weight from your shoulders, stress
washes away from your body and spirit.

Open yourself to God's peace and rest in the tranquil
and rejuvenating waters of his care for you.

*O God: I rely on your divine strength. Let me give to
you the burdens of my heart. Provide for me your
soothing, rejuvenating rest. Amen.*

Cast all your anxiety on him
because he cares for you.

1 PETER 5:7 NIV

EVERYDAY CHOICES

*Choose life, that both you and
your descendants may live.*
DEUTERONOMY 30:19 NKJV

Most of us spend time thinking and weighing options
before making important decisions, but we often forget
the significance of choices we make every day—our

words, our actions and reactions,
our attitude and our outlook.

Consider God's life-giving choices.
His compassion shines in you
when you opt for the gentle word
and kindly gesture, even when
tempers flare. His effective work is reflected in your productive choices, those choices that build up and bring
about positive change, and his peace flows through your
faithful efforts to maintain harmony between you and
others.

God's presence shows when your small, everyday choices
reflect his Spirit's work in your heart.

*Dear God: As you have chosen me to follow you, help me
make godly and life-affirming decisions and
choices in all I do each day. Amen.*

I bless the LORD who gives me counsel.

PSALM 16:7 NRSV

TO THE FINISH

Think of a time you continued with a difficult task until you completed it. In all likelihood, you determined to see it through because you kept a goal in mind—a good

grade, praise, or simply the satisfaction of a job well done. Your perseverance had a reward.

Your growth in God is a lifelong project, and God has put a goal in front of you to encourage you to carry it to the finish. He assures you of everlasting life with him and the reward of his approval. He promises not only to offer you hope for today but to show you the heavenly result of remaining faithful to him.

Dear God: When the way you have prepared for me seems difficult, remind me of the blessings you have in store for those who persevere to the end. Amen.

Jesus said, "I'll make each conqueror a pillar in the sanctuary of my God, a permanent position of honor.

REVELATION 3:12 MSG

UPWARD ACTION

*Since we are receiving a kingdom which cannot be
shaken, let us have grace, by which we may serve
God acceptably with reverence and godly fear.*
HEBREWS 12:28 NKJV

In a relationship, love expresses itself in acts of kindness,
thoughtfulness, and devotion. The same holds true for
the relationship between you and God.

In the Bible, Jesus asks you to love God
with your whole being and to put him
above everyone and everything else.
When you do so, you will want to obey
him by responding to his Word and acting
on those things you know he requires of
you, simply for the sake of pleasing him.

As you grow in love and service, cultivating and using
the gifts God has given you, your relationship will show
all the signs of genuine love.

*Dear God: Grant that I may learn to love you more,
grow in obedience, and use for your service
the gifts you have given to me. Amen.*

OUTWARD ACTION

Serve wholeheartedly, as if you were serving the
Lord, not men, because you know that the Lord will
reward everyone for whatever good he does.
EPHESIANS 6:7–8 NIV

When you consider what you do each day, you might
imagine you're limited in your ability to serve others.
Not so!

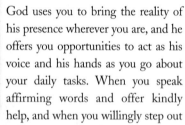

God uses you to bring the reality of
his presence wherever you are, and he
offers you opportunities to act as his
voice and his hands as you go about
your daily tasks. When you speak
affirming words and offer kindly
help, and when you willingly step out
to assist those in need or support worthy causes, you are
serving others.

Take a moment to reflect on how you can serve others
today, and you will find as many ways as there are godly
thoughts, desires, words, and actions.

O God: Fill me with desire to serve others in the things I
do and say to help those in need. Open my eyes and heart
to the opportunities before me today. Amen.

If anyone serves, he should do it with the strength God provides, so that in all things God may be praised through Jesus Christ.

1 PETER 4:11 NIV

Embracing

GODLY LOVE

*Live a life of love, just as Christ loved us and
gave himself up for us as a fragrant
offering and sacrifice to God.*
EPHESIANS 5:2 NIV

When we speak with one another about love, we're often
talking about sex, emotions, and feelings. When God

talks about love, he has in
mind a far more powerful,
more encompassing, and more
lasting kind of love.

Biblical love reflects God's
attitude toward you, a disposition rooted in his selfless
decision to be and remain in
love with you. His unchangeable feelings for you mean
your relationship with him is one of eternal stability, and
his love a worthy dwelling place for your feelings of gratitude, joy, and love.

In his eternal embrace, you know true love, and God
invites you to share his attitude of love with others.

*Dear God: As I become more aware of your feelings
toward me, allow your committed and selfless love
to permeate all my relationships. Amen.*

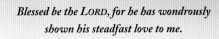

Blessed be the LORD, for he has wondrously
shown his steadfast love to me.

PSALM 31:21 NRSV

HAPPINESS FOR A LIFETIME

*God gives wisdom, knowledge, and
joy to those who please him.*
ECCLESIASTES 2:26 NLT

As you turn your thoughts to God, you realize more and more that the happiness the world brings you creates temporary contentment, at best.

God intends for you to have a lifetime of happiness, so he has sent his Spirit to live in your heart. His Spirit produces joy, an inner joy neither dampened nor discouraged by outward events and circumstances. Assured that you belong to God, with your reliance firmly planted in his strength and your trust resolutely set on his promises, you can take hold of genuine happiness.

It's free, it comes from God, and it's yours to keep forever.

Heavenly Father: Grant me the courage to reach out and take hold of the joy you have in store for me, because I desire a joyful heart and happy spirit. Amen.

*I will greatly rejoice in the L*ORD*, my*
soul shall be joyful in my God.

ISAIAH 61:10 NKJV

ONE STORY

You shall know the truth, and the
truth shall make you free.
JOHN 8:32 NKJV

Imagine hearing a story from one friend, then hearing a different account from another friend. You realize because you didn't witness the actual event, you may never know what really happened.

God understands the limitations of human reason and experience and has given you a way to know the facts of his work on Earth, his love for you, and his promise of heaven. He provides the Bible as a means of opening spiritual truths to you. As you read or hear it, his Spirit informs your heart and mind of facts you can discover no other way than through his Word.

With God, you have one story—the true story.

Heavenly Father: Turn my attention to you and your
Word as I search for the truth about you and your
ways among people and in my life. Amen.

*Your lovingkindness is before my eyes,
and I have walked in Your truth.*

PSALM 26:3 NKJV

LIBERATION

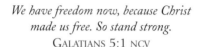

*We have freedom now, because Christ
made us free. So stand strong.*
GALATIANS 5:1 NCV

The women's liberation movement of the 1970s brought
about remarkable gains for women in education,
employment, and legal rights. Few of us would willingly
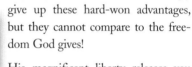
give up these hard-won advantages,
but they cannot compare to the freedom God gives!

His magnificent liberty releases you
from guilt, fear, and self-gratification
and allows you to experience complete
harmony of body and soul. His freedom lets you move ahead in spiritual
maturity and holy living, and by his authority you can
count yourself as a worthy and purposeful child of God.

Celebrate your freedom today by exploring some of the
most meaningful advantages of heart, mind, and soul
that Jesus won for you.

*Dear God: Thank you for winning for me true freedom,
freedom of the spirit. Release me from anything that
threatens my priceless liberty in you. Amen.*

*Where the Spirit of the
Lord is, there is freedom.*

2 CORINTHIANS 3:17 NCV

RESPONSIBLE ACTION

Let your light shine before men in such a way that they may see your good works, and glorify your Father who is in heaven.

MATTHEW 5:16 NASB

We know what it's like to begin an exercise program with high hopes, then find our energy flag as time passes.

Without continued motivation, we're likely to quit and not reach our desired goal.

While God has provided your salvation, he warns you not to lose sight of it by becoming neglectful of your faith or taking it for granted. He reminds you to remain a responsible possessor of faith by exercising it in words and actions reflective of his presence in your life. In so doing, you win others to God by your conduct and you become a godly presence in a world in need of his peace and love.

Heavenly Father: In gratitude for the promise of eternal life, I want to live in a way worthy of the fine gift you have seen fit to give me. Amen.

*It is God who works in you
to will and to act according
to his good purpose.*

PHILIPPIANS 2:13 NIV

EYES WIDE OPEN

What happens when we live God's way?...
We find ourselves involved in loyal commitments.
GALATIANS 5:22, 23 MSG

When you make a pledge to another person, you know every moment of every day will not be rosy. If it were, the pledge would not be meaningful. You count on  experiencing times of joy and sadness, satisfaction and frustration, but your pledge takes precedence over all and keeps you going.

Your commitment to God requires the same understanding. You must accept what will happen—you will find delight, despair, and everything in between. For this reason, Jesus advises his disciples to count the cost before making a promise to follow him. Know, though, that you can count on him to be there for you every step of the way.

Dear God: Instill in me a willingness to give up
anything preventing me from giving myself
wholeheartedly to your Spirit. I commit
myself to you. Amen.

The eyes of the LORD range throughout the earth to strengthen those whose hearts are fully committed to him.

2 CHRONICLES 16:9 NIV

WHO I AM

Love from the center of who you are; don't fake it.
ROMANS 12:9 MSG

Many girls are taught to hide their true feelings behind a mask of pleasantries, and when they grow into womanhood, many continue their charade of benevolent

words and acts. The mere surface appearance of goodness, however, is not enough.

God sees through masks of any kind, and he reads what's really in our heart. Where he finds negative thoughts or cunning motives, he brings about a change of heart so

the mask can disappear, allowing genuine goodness to create affection, kindliness, and thoughtfulness to others.

The harmony God works between private feelings and public behavior enables you to be forever free to show your true face to the world.

Heavenly Father: Fill me with your Spirit so my love for others will be genuine and my words and actions an authentic reflection of who I am in you. Amen.

Love one another deeply, from the heart.

1 PETER 1:22 NIV

GOOD REASONS

I will hope continually, and will
praise you yet more and more.
PSALM 71:14 NRSV

"I hope" reflects a wish, but when the Bible speaks of hope, the word refers to a conviction that God's promises are true.

 When God's Spirit plants hope in your heart, you perceive your life in light of his purpose for you. You rely on his promise to protect you, guide you, forgive you, and bring you at last to live with him in heaven. Your conviction gives you cause for optimism even when things aren't going your way, because you have placed your hope in God's power and his pledge to work all things to your good.

Take hold of hope and make it the light of your life.

Dear God: Strengthen my belief in your words and grant
me sure and certain hope in your plan of salvation and
promise of eternal life. Amen.

My soul claims the Lord as my inheritance;
therefore I will hope in him.

LAMENTATIONS 3:24 TLB

ALLOW FOR CHANGE

*To everything there is a season, a time
for every purpose under heaven.*
ECCLESIASTES 3:1 NKJV

Women experience change intimately, changing from girl-hood to maturity and from fertility to menopause. Rarely do we welcome change with open arms. God, who put in

place the seasons of nature and the stages of a woman's life, offers another perspective.

Changes in your life, whether initiated by you or by other factors, invite you to discover God in deeper and rewarding ways. Changes shake up your status quo and send you seeking a new level of comfort. When your searching leads you closer to God, your times of change build your courage and strength.

Resist the urge to run. Embrace change instead as a way to know God better.

Dear God: When I go through times of change, help me choose a positive, productive response and grant me contentment with each new phase in my life. Amen.

God changes times and seasons

DANIEL 2:21 NIV

GOD'S MESSAGE

*Laugh with your happy friends when they're happy;
share tears when they're down. Get along with
each other. . . . Discover beauty in everyone.*
ROMANS 12:14 MSG

Ads on television and in fashion magazines reinforce a beguiling but false message: for true happiness, pamper

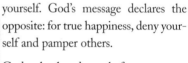

yourself. God's message declares the opposite: for true happiness, deny yourself and pamper others.

God, who loved you before you were born and continues to love you and preserve your life today, never stops giving himself to you. When Jesus was born, he denied himself the glory and luxury

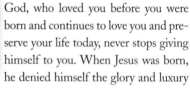

of heaven to carry out his part of God's plan for salvation, and he ultimately gave his life for the sake of yours.

God's Spirit in you prompts you to listen to his message: If you desire happiness for yourself, lavish it wholeheartedly on others.

*Dear God: Help me overcome the natural desire to
indulge myself instead of serving the needs of others.
Plant unselfish giving deep in my heart. Amen.*

Present your bodies as a living sacrifice, holy and acceptable to God, which is your spiritual worship.

ROMANS 12:1 NRSV

SONG OF THANKS

Overflowing grace God has given to you. Thank God for this gift too wonderful for words
2 CORINTHIANS 9:14–15 NLT

When the prophetess Miriam led the Israelites in song, she proclaimed how God had worked to deliver his people from oppression. To this day, gratitude to God stems  from an awareness of the great things he has done and continues to do.

Through the ministry of Jesus, God delivered you from the oppression of earthly desires and the chains of cynicism, guilt, and unbelief. He made available the assurance of his mercy and compassion, and he opened to you the knowledge of his willingness to call you his own and lead you on a path of holiness. This is his utmost desire.

In thanksgiving, let your life proclaim his wonderful work!

Heavenly Father: Thank you for all you have done and continue to do in my life. Let me respond with a heart of gratitude and with words of thanks and praise. Amen.

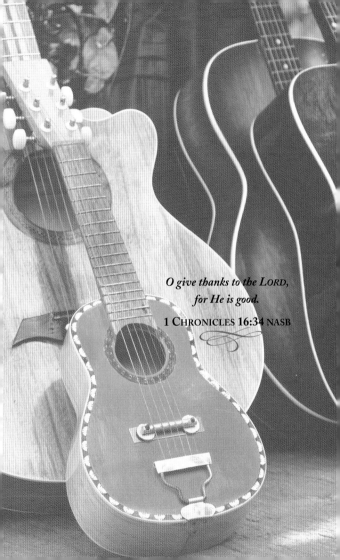

*O give thanks to the Lord,
for He is good.*

1 Chronicles 16:34 NASB

REALLY CLEAN

Happy are those who live pure lives,
who follow the LORD's teachings.
PSALM 119:1 NCV

As a teenager, you probably thought about the concept of purity of life in terms of saving sexual relations until marriage. While the idea of purity of life certainly

includes sexual morality, it encompasses far more than a single aspect of a woman's life.

God's idea of purity directs your thoughts to subjects of worth and value that give birth to words and actions consistent with God's commandments. The kind of purity God has in mind for you isn't afraid to confront the world's loose morals with boldness, because its foundation is in the power of God's eternal truth.

Genuine purity begins in the heart washed clean by God's Spirit.

Dear God: Grant me the resolve to see where I need to
increase in purity, and instill in me the willingness to
allow your cleansing Spirit to wash me in holiness. Amen.

Oh, worship the LORD in the beauty of holiness!

1 CHRONICLES 16:29 NKJV

BEEN THERE, DONE THAT

There are many rooms in my Father's house. . . .
I am going there to prepare a place for you.
JOHN 14:2 NCV

When the subject turns to motherhood, women who are mothers speak up, while those without children remain silent. On the subject of heaven, however, non-

experienced people have no qualms about speaking out on the topic!

During his earthly ministry, Jesus could speak about heaven with full authority because he had been there and he knew he was going to return there. He spoke with experience, having seen the glories of heaven, the angels, and all God's beloved people gathered around. He described what it looks like and what you can expect when you get to your heavenly home.

When the subject comes to heaven, listen to the expert—Jesus.

Dear Lord: Thank you for the promise of heaven, and keep me listening to Jesus, the only one qualified to tell me about the peace and joy awaiting me there. Amen.

He puts a little of heaven in our hearts
so that we'll never settle for less.

2 CORINTHIANS 5:5 MSG

A WISE WOMAN

Wisdom is a tree of life to those who embrace her;
happy are those who hold her tightly.
PROVERBS 3:18 NLT

We equate wisdom with remarkable perception and
insight earned through experience. We often attribute
wisdom to grandmothers who have overcome a lifetime

of hardships with grace and
courage. God, however, opens
wisdom to all, regardless of age
and situation in life.

When you study and meditate on
God's Word, you gain understanding and you begin to learn more
and more about the relationship
he desires to have with you. You start to look beyond
what your physical eyes can see and what your human
reason can comprehend. You begin to grasp things of the
Spirit made understandable only through the Spirit.

Today, let God make you a wise woman.

Heavenly Father: Teach me those things known only by
you so I may gain knowledge of the spirit and wisdom of
the heart. I desire to become wise in your ways. Amen.

*Women who have lived wisely and well will shine
brilliantly, like the cloudless, star-strewn night skies.*

DANIEL 12:3 MSG

Becoming

DAUGHTER OF GOD

Do everything without complaining or arguing
so that you may become blameless
and pure, children of God.
PHILIPPIANS 2:14–15 NIV

If you're a mother, you've heard it—"Do I have to?" As a child, you probably said it yourself. A child's rebellion is

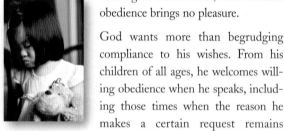 nothing to boast about, and resentful obedience brings no pleasure.

God wants more than begrudging compliance to his wishes. From his children of all ages, he welcomes willing obedience when he speaks, including those times when the reason he makes a certain request remains unclear, or when the particular sacrifice he asks of you seems difficult and burdensome.

When you eagerly listen to God's voice and gladly carry out his requests, you're a child of God giving your heavenly Father something to be pleased about.

Heavenly Father: Grant me a heart of willing
submission to your will and a sincere desire to
please you as your obedient daughter. Amen.

Just look at it—we're called children of God!
That's who we really are.

1 JOHN 3:1 MSG

WOMAN OF PRAYER

Whatever you ask for in prayer with faith,
you will receive.
MATTHEW 21:22 NRSV

We know communication builds healthy relationships,
and most of us go to great lengths to maintain open
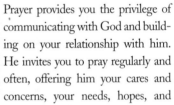
interaction between ourselves and
our loved ones.

Prayer provides you the privilege of
communicating with God and building on your relationship with him.
He invites you to pray regularly and
often, offering him your cares and
concerns, your needs, hopes, and
desires. Even though he already knows everything you're
telling him, he also knows you need to articulate your
thoughts to him, your loving friend and generous provider.

Communication being a two-way street, he speaks to
you through Scripture. The more you listen, the more
you know how to pray.

Dear God: I pray that our lines of communication will
always be open. Thank you for hearing me. I truly
desire to become a woman of prayer. Amen.

When you call on me, when you come and pray to me, I'll
listen. When you come looking for me, you'll find me.

JEREMIAH 29:12–13 MSG

FILLED WITH WISDOM

*If any of you lacks wisdom, he should ask God, who
gives generously to all without finding fault,
and it will be given to him.*
JAMES 1:5 NIV

No matter how knowledgeable a woman may appear,
not one of us can claim competence in all circumstances.

Sooner or later we're faced with a
problem, a situation, or a stage in
life in which we have to admit we're
helpless.

When you're at a loss for answers,
God welcomes your admission of
need, because your realization of
your human inadequacy allows God
to fill you with his wisdom. He wants to lavish on you
his understanding so you can discern his will and his
solutions, and most of all, enjoy his transcendent peace.

Offer your limitations to him and receive his boundless
wisdom in return.

*Dear God: When I'm most at a loss to know what to do,
place in me a heart open to your wisdom, the source
of all knowledge and truth. Amen.*

There's nothing better than being wise, knowing how to interpret the meaning of life.

ECCLESIASTES **8:1** MSG

WHAT EVERY WOMAN WANTS

*I will be with them in trouble. I will
rescue and honor them.*
PSALM 91:15 NLT

God has placed within you a deep desire to be honored
and respected. Every woman feels it. The great Aretha
Franklin even sang about it—R-E-S-P-E-C-T. But so

often we think we have to
demand it. Those who try
soon find themselves frustrated and disappointed.

True honor comes from
God. It's his gift contained
in his great love. As you respond, it becomes his reward
for living in accordance with his will. It's his way of saying you have pleased him, blessed him, and made him
proud.

Forget about seeking honor from others. The honor that
comes from God will satisfy you to the depths of your
soul.

*Dear God: Thank you for honoring me with your love.
Teach me to honor you with my life. Amen.*

*Worthy are You, our Lord and our God,
to receive glory and honor and power.*

REVELATION 4:11 NASB

TOUCH A LIFE

Do not repay evil with evil or insult with insult,
but with blessing, because to this you were
called so that you may inherit a blessing.
1 PETER 3:9 NIV

Think of a woman who has touched your life in a particular way. She may have shown you a special kindness

or helped you during a difficult time in your life, choosing to devote her time to you along with everything else vying for her attention.

Being a blessing to others means putting their needs before your own, gladly and willingly listening, helping, and comforting. You may hear a

thank-you at the time, or only later when the person realizes how much you helped, or maybe not at all—but you will certainly hear it from the lips of Jesus, who works through you to bless the lives of others.

Dear God: Wherever my day takes me,
grant that I may touch lives for good.
As you have blessed me, I have
resolved to bless others. Amen.

*Become the kind of container God can use
to present any and every kind of gift to
his guests for their blessing.*

2 TIMOTHY 2:21 MSG

HEART'S PEACE

Peacemakers who sow in peace raise a
harvest of righteousness.
JAMES 3:18 NIV

Though you may not be in a position to call an end to all wars, God still places on you the mantle of peacemaker.

God knows true peace begins in the human heart, so he grants you his peace and the insight you need to live in harmony with who you are and the life he has given you. To make peace with the past, you have his forgiveness, and to know peace today and every day, you possess his strength and wisdom.

Your deep conviction of God's peace works harmony among those around you. There's something about peace that catches on, one heart at a time.

Heavenly Father: Help me know your peace even in the
midst of struggle. Grant me harmony of heart and soul
so I can become your instrument of peace. Amen.

*How beautiful upon the mountains are the feet of
the messenger who announces peace.*

ISAIAH 52:7 NRSV

FOLLOW THE LEADER

Servants must be reverent before the mystery of the faith,
not using their position to try to run things.

1 TIMOTHY 3:9 MSG

More and more women occupy leadership positions in
the corporate world, in the community, and in politics.
As a child of God, you possess the status of a servant-

 leader, and the require-
ments of a leader apply to
you.

Leaders step out in front of
the crowd instead of wor-
rying about what everyone
else is doing, and so must

you when you look to God's rules and his expectations.
Leaders look beyond today's wants for tomorrow's needs
and take responsible action even when subject to the
doubts and opposition of others. True servant-leaders
live in a way worthy of emulation, and by example, guide
others to God.

Dear God: By following you, I am stepping out from the
crowd. Grant me your strength and boldness so my
life can lead others to you. Amen.

The Lord will go ahead of you,
and he, the God of Israel, will
protect you from behind.

ISAIAH 52:12 TLB

HEART OF MERCY

God's mercy goes on from generation to generation, to all who reverence him.
LUKE 1:50 TLB

An act of mercy includes offering practical help to people in need, but it doesn't end there. God set the standard for mercy when he embraced humanity with a heart of compassion and tender care.

God's mercy on you means you have his protection, his forgiveness, and his help for your every need. This is the kind of compassion he models for you to show others, a compassion marked by attentive care for the needs of others, unconditional pardon for the offenses of others, and quiet forgiveness for the omissions of others.

Your heart of compassion should pour out mercy with unreserved generosity.

Heavenly Father: Let your continuing compassion motivate my words, acts, and attitude of mercy toward others, especially the weak and needy. Amen.

Jesus said: "Have mercy, just as your Father has mercy."

LUKE 6:36 NIrV

ROLE MODEL

*Be an example to the believers with your words, your
actions, your love, your faith, and your pure life.*
1 TIMOTHY 4:12 NCV

In our formative years, the women we chose as role
models influenced how we perceived ourselves and the
goals we set for ourselves. Now, as adults, we are the ones
younger women watch.

God reminds you that your appearance and behavior matter, because
he understands how influential you
are to those around you, especially
young women still discovering their
own personalities and priorities. As
a role model, the way you carry
yourself reflects your values, and the words you use in
everyday conversation declare your attitude toward God
and other people.

You were created not only to please God but also to reflect
his virtue and demonstrate his goodness and purity.

*Dear God: Help me conduct myself in a manner worthy
of emulation, especially for those in need of an
example of godly womanhood. Amen.*

In all things show them how to live by your life.

TITUS 2:7 NLV

BONDS OF FRIENDSHIP

A true friend is closer than your own family.
PROVERBS 18:24 CEV

You are blessed indeed if you have a friend you can call in a time of crisis and know she will be there for you. She is the kind of friend God intends for you, and the kind of friend he empowers you to be as well.

True companionship and friendship develops as you go out of your way to support and comfort others. Your constancy allows others to place their trust in you, and your sharing of thoughtfulness, helpfulness, and a listening ear forge the bonds of genuine and lasting friendship.

God has called himself your friend, and he has opened the blessing of friendship to you.

Dear God: Thank you for the gift of friendship. Help me to be an attentive and appreciative friend, especially when I'm called on to help in a time of need. Amen.

A friend loves at all times. She is there
to help when trouble comes

PROVERBS 17:17 NIrV

HEART'S TREASURES

*Be diligent to present yourself approved to God,
a worker who does not need to be ashamed,
rightly dividing the word of truth.*
2 TIMOTHY 2:15 NKJV

In the scriptural account of Jesus' birth, we read how his
mother, Mary, took in all the signs and wonders around
her and treasured them in her heart.

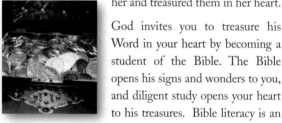

God invites you to treasure his
Word in your heart by becoming a
student of the Bible. The Bible
opens his signs and wonders to you,
and diligent study opens your heart
to his treasures. Bible literacy is an
important element of your walk with God. Through it,
you will discover the deeper meanings in Scripture as you
see how each piece fits together to assure you of his love,
forgiveness, and salvation found in Jesus.

*Dear God: Help me become a faithful
student of your Word by instilling in me
a heart ready and eager to treasure your
eternal truths. Amen.*

Great peace have they who love your law, and
nothing can make them stumble.

PSALM 119:165 NIV

JOYFUL WAITING

May the God of hope fill you with all joy and peace
in believing, that you may abound in hope
by the power of the Holy Spirit.
ROMANS 15:13 NKJV

The prophetess Anna was a devout woman who spent her long widowhood in joyful expectation of the prom-

ised redeemer. God rewarded her with the privilege of seeing the infant Jesus and recognizing him as Savior. Anna gave God heartfelt thanks and praise.

When you read and meditate on God's promises to you, he offers you the motivation to live in joyful expectation

of their fulfillment. His Spirit, a Spirit of hope, empowers you to rely on what God has already accomplished in your life and to patiently wait on things not yet seen.

In joyful expectation as you await the fruition of his promises, give him heartfelt thanks and praise.

Heavenly Father: The wondrous promises you have
made known to me in your Word create a spirit
of joyful expectation in me. Amen.

Let praise cascade off my lips;
after all, you've taught me
the truth about life!

PSALM 119:172 MSG

MAKING OF A SAINT

Train yourself in godliness.
1 TIMOTHY 4:7 NRSV

While holiness sounds like an ethereal concept reserved for the rarefied air of a convent, it's actually a down-to-earth, observable, and practicable lifestyle. It's the lifestyle God has in mind for you.

God educates you in the ways of holiness as you read the Bible and allow his Spirit to enter those places in your heart and life needing light and warmth. He helps you use the experiences and conditions that you encounter daily to bring you toward a more complete and thorough holiness and godly stature.

If you haven't already guessed, God is preparing you for sainthood, because in Jesus you're a saint in his eyes right now.

Heavenly Father: You have put before me all I need to live the life of a saint. Train me in your ways and help me become a true example of godliness to others. Amen.

Pursue a righteous life—a life of wonder,
faith, love, steadiness, courtesy.

1 TIMOTHY 6:11 MSG

LIFELONG LEARNING

Let us leave the elementary teachings about
Christ and go on to maturity.
HEBREWS 6:1 NIV

Many women consider themselves lifelong learners. No matter how many years they have been out of school, these women eagerly examine new subjects and readily welcome new knowledge and discoveries.

In calling you to faith, God has put you on a path of lifelong learning. After you accept his plan of salvation, God invites you to explore his many mysteries and delve more deeply into his treasury of biblical wisdom. He encourages you to let your questions take you even further into his Word, because in finding answers you grow in faith.

Spend your lifetime having the time of your life learning about him.

Dear God: I want to continue to learn about you and the
truths you have put before me. I desire to become a
knowledgeable and mature Christian. Amen.

*Teach the righteous and they
will gain in learning.*

Proverbs 9:9 nrsv

Walking

WORDS OF LOVE

*Christ's love ... has the first and last
word in everything we do.*
2 Corinthians 5:14 MSG

God wants you to have the first word—and the last word
too. When you approach your day with an attitude of
loving-kindness toward the people you meet and the

tasks you perform, every
word you speak refreshes
and renews those relationships like a gentle spring
rain. Your speech plants the
seeds of kindness, and your
actions cultivate harmony and understanding between
people. When you close your day with the same mind-
set, the last things you say leave behind God's blessing
and the sweet fragrance of his peace.

When you walk in relationship with God, love is the first
word and the last word, and they both belong to you.

*Dear God: In my walk with you, help me learn the great
power of your love at work through me in everything
I say and do today. Amen.*

Pleasing words are like honey. They are sweet to the soul and healing to the bones.

PROVERBS 16:24 NLV

SOUL-DEEP JOY

The joy of the LORD is your strength!
NEHEMIAH 8:10 NLT

Chemotherapy had taken its toll on her hair, weight, and energy, yet her friends could not help but notice the aura of transcendent joy emanating from deep within one remarkable woman. The reason was her trust in God.

The joy of the Lord, understandable when times are good, startles when its presence persists, even increases when the days turn difficult. This is the kind of joy God has for you, a joy you hold on to that astonishes people as it continues to deepen and strengthen despite hardships and regardless of adverse circumstances.

Nothing has the power to steal from you the soul-deep joy that is yours in God.

Heavenly Father: In all things, let me
rejoice in your great love and put my
trust in you, and let my happiness
find its home in you alone. Amen.

You will live in joy and peace. The mountains
and hills, the trees of the field—all the
world around you—will rejoice.

ISAIAH 55:12 TLB

HOW TO BE BEAUTIFUL

Those who walk uprightly enter into peace.
ISAIAH 57:2 NIV

Genuine beauty grows from a peaceful soul. Inner harmony leaves a woman's face free of tension, and her mind and heart free to love and care for others.

 As you continue to obey God's commandments and discover his will, you will notice a difference in how you feel and how you look. Your peace, a peace possible only from a clear conscience and a reliance on God's power in your life, transforms you. You feel in harmony with yourself, and you find your tranquility reflected in the mirror.

Your friends may remark on your sparkling eyes or your welcoming smile, but what they're really seeing is your beautiful soul.

Dear God: I yearn for the beauty possessed by women at peace with themselves and secure in their relationship with you. Give me a soul immersed in you! Amen.

The fruit of righteousness will be peace; the effect of righteousness will be quietness and confidence forever.

ISAIAH 32:17 NIV

PLANNED KINDNESS

Do what is right and true. Be kind
and merciful to each other.
ZECHARIAH 7:9 NCV

"Practice random acts of kindness," a catch-phrase of the mid-1990s, describes a good deed done for a stranger with no thought of receiving anything in return. God

goes beyond random acts when he pours out his kindness on those he loves.

When you give your heart to him, kindness becomes a way of life for you, because your realization of his eternal and intentional kindness toward you makes any other response impossible. Your kindness, a reflection of his to you, touches strangers and permeates your deepest relationships. It demonstrates its presence in the countless acts of caring and words you offer in support and encouragement to others.

Dear God: Each day, help me choose kindness in my
dealings with others, remembering the extraordinary
kindness you have shown me. Amen.

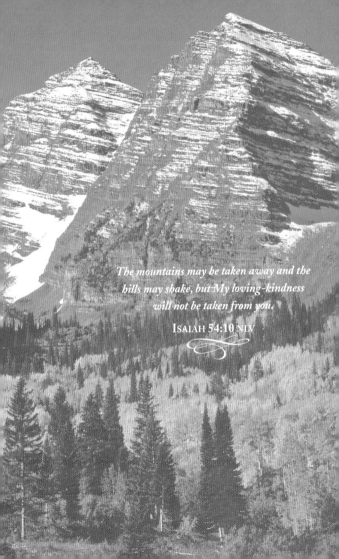

The mountains may be taken away and the
hills may shake, but My loving-kindness
will not be taken from you.

ISAIAH 54:10 NLV

POWER OF GENTLENESS

Be gentle with one another, sensitive.
EPHESIANS 4:32 MSG

Many women dismiss the quality of gentleness as an outmoded virtue impractical in today's world where they earn their own living, work alongside men, seek promotions, and negotiate the purchase price of their house  and car. No one knows better than God the realities of your life, and he still calls you to wrap yourself in gentleness. Jesus, God's supreme example of gentleness, possessed all the powers of God, yet chose compassion, forgiveness, and tenderness in his dealings with humble women and men.

In Jesus, you have your mentor and every reason to bring the quality of godly gentleness as a positive attribute into the twenty-first century.

Heavenly Father: Grant me sensitivity to the needs of others, a compassionate heart and a temperate tongue. Let your Spirit enable me to practice the power of gentleness. Amen.

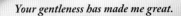

Your gentleness has made me great.

PSALM 18:35 NKJV

FOLLOW IN FAITH

We walk by faith, not by sight.
2 CORINTHIANS 5:7 NKJV

She wanted to learn how to make a quilt, so she bought a book on quilting. How each step contributed to the finished quilt was not always clear to her, but she

followed instructions and completed a beautiful work of art.

As you continue to walk with God, some steps along the way may seem unclear, and that's when God asks you to proceed in faith. He shows you his plan—ultimately life with him in heaven—and in the Bible he gives you his step-by-step instructions on how to get there and live a God-pleasing life along the way.

Continue in faith, and God promises you a beautiful result.

Dear God: Grant me the desire and willingness to walk in faith and follow the Bible's teachings so I may rejoice in the fulfillment of all your promises. Amen.

*Faith is the substance of things hoped for,
the evidence of things not seen*

HEBREWS **11:1** NKJV

HE'S NEVER LATE

Be patient ... until the Lord's coming.
JAMES 5:7 NIV

"The patience of Job" didn't apply to his wife, for as Job endured extraordinary trials, she saw only his wretchedness and even advised her husband to give up the strug-

gle and die. Though the Bible says Job cried out to God in distress, he did not give up, viewing his trials through the lens of eternity.

God opens his ears to your cries and his arms when you hurt, and above all, he opens your eyes so you can see things from his perspective. When you place this moment against all eternity, your Spirit-given patience deepens because you see God bringing all things to pass, and he is never late.

Dear God: When I feel frustrated, send your Spirit into my heart and grant me patience to endure, relying on you to work each situation out in your own time. Amen.

God will strengthen you with his own great power.
And you will not give up when troubles come,
but you will be patient.

COLOSSIANS 1:11 ICB

GIFT OF FORGIVENESS

Bear with one another and, if anyone has a complaint against another, forgive each other; just as the Lord has forgiven you, so you also must forgive.
COLOSSIANS 3:13 NRSV

God has provided complete forgiveness through the work of Christ, and now he asks you to follow his example when it comes to those who have hurt you.

In his earthly ministry, Jesus Christ bore the insults of his persecutors without returning insult for insult, and he uttered words of forgiveness even to the soldiers nailing him to the cross. He never considered whether the person deserved forgiveness; he simply forgave, because his compassionate heart allowed no other response.

Take pleasure in living as the completely forgiven woman of God you are, and let your heart of compassion deal mercifully with those in need of your pardon.

Heavenly Father: In gratitude for the gift of your forgiveness, move me to choose forgiveness instead of offense when dealing with the failings of others. Amen.

Love prospers when a fault is forgiven.

PROVERBS 17:9 NLT

SAFETY FIRST

My people will live in safety,
and no one will frighten them.

EZEKIEL 34:28 NLT

Safety becomes a primary concern when a woman examines toys for her young children or helps her elderly parents choose an apartment. Similarly, God has your safety in mind as he guides you on the path of life.

God keeps you safe from harmful influences by reminding you not only of his love for you but of the purpose he has for you. He keeps you secure in the knowledge of your status as a beloved woman of God, and he establishes in you the Spirit-grown conviction that you have nothing to fear.

Privileged to live a life of meaning and purpose, rest securely in him.

Dear God: Help me find my sole security in you
and your divine purpose for my life. I rest
at ease in the strong shelter of
your love. Amen.

The beloved of the L ORD rests in safety

D EUTERONOMY 33:12 NRSV

YOU ARE NOT ALONE

If we live in the light, as God is in the light,
we can share fellowship with each other.
1 JOHN 1:7 NCV

As you walk forward in your relationship with God, it's important to spend time with others who share your  faith. Churches, women's Bible study groups, service projects, and social circles all provide opportunities. You may be surprised how quickly you bond and how deep and lasting your relationships become. After all, you share a secret, the greatest love of all!

Surround yourself with women who love and respect God, and you will soon find they can be a source of true wisdom and spiritual encouragement. Your heavenly Father never intended for you to walk the life of faith alone, but rather with other women who will love and support you.

Heavenly Father: Help me to find friends who are
women of faith. Grant me many opportunities to
join in fellowship with them. Amen.

Love the brothers and sisters of God's family.

1 PETER 2:17 NCV

TOGETHER AS ONE

*May the God who gives endurance and
encouragement give you a spirit of unity
among yourselves as you follow Christ Jesus.*
ROMANS 15:5 NIV

A family living together in harmony and the family of
believers worshiping together in peace meet God's

intentions for his people. Good
things happen when Christians
come together in heart and
mind—families become havens of
encouragement, support, and affir-
mation, and congregations grow
into models of true Christian unity.

God invites you to help implement his vision of unity in
both your natural and your spiritual families. He sends
his Spirit, empowering you to discover and develop areas
of common interest and purpose, and he sets in front of
you his ideal of a unified people of God, offering you an
inspiring picture of the goal he has in mind.

*Dear God: Put before my eyes your desire for all believers
to journey together within the common embrace
of Christian love. Amen.*

How very good and pleasant it is when kindred live together in unity!

PSALM 133:1 NRSV

WHOLE YOU

*May God himself, the God who makes everything
holy and whole, make you holy and whole, put you
together—spirit, soul, and body.*
1 THESSALONIANS 5:23 MSG

God has been called the Great Physician for good reason—wherever he finds a broken spirit, he works to heal and make things whole again.

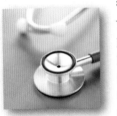

Your innermost private wounds are known by God, and you cannot hide them from his restorative touch. Instead, he draws you close to him, caressing you with the balm of his comfort, bathing you in the cleansing waters of forgiveness, and embracing you in complete wholeness of spirit and soul.

Whenever your heart weeps because of wounds from the past or sorrows suffered today, step close to God, the Great Physician of body and soul. He will heal you.

*Great Physician: There are broken places in my life,
and I need your creative and re-creative touch
for the wholeness only you have the power to
bring about in my life. Amen.*

I am the LORD who heals you.

EXODUS 15:26 NKJV

TRUE VINE

*Whoever pursues righteousness and kindness
will find life and honor.*
PROVERBS 21:21 NRSV

To her consternation, a gardener discovered a climbing weed had entangled itself in a favored vine. The only way she could tell the weed from the vine was by examining the leaves.

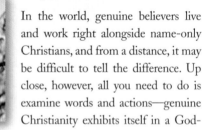

In the world, genuine believers live and work right alongside name-only Christians, and from a distance, it may be difficult to tell the difference. Up close, however, all you need to do is examine words and actions—genuine Christianity exhibits itself in a God-pleasing lifestyle and an obvious desire to grow in Christlikeness.

Take a few moments to consider how the "leaves" of your life reveal you belong to Jesus, who has said, "I am the vine."

*Dear God: Cultivate in me a sincere desire to walk in
uprightness of heart so my words and actions
will show I belong to you. Amen.*

The ways of right-living people glow with light;
the longer they live, the brighter they shine.

PROVERBS 4:18 MSG

EXPERIENCE HIS SPIRIT

We have not received the spirit of the world but the Spirit who is from God, that we may understand what God has freely given us.
1 CORINTHIANS 2:12 NIV

Imagine strolling on a woodland path and discovering a small bench nestled among the trees. As you sit for a few

moments, the breathtaking peace of the forest comes over you and infuses your soul with its sweetness. You're humbled by the honor of being who you are in this time and place.

As you walk in relationship with God, there will be moments when you're stirred by a startling awareness of the Holy Spirit living, breathing, and working in you. The humbling experience leaves you without words to express your new understanding, but with a deeper conviction that God has, indeed, chosen you to be his dwelling place.

Dear God: Grant me faithfulness on my walk with your Spirit, and open me to the humbling awareness of you in my heart and in my life. Amen.

*Do you not know that your body is a temple of the
Holy Spirit who is in you, whom you have from God?*

1 Corinthians 6:19 nasb

Enjoying

JOY OF SALVATION

*God declared us righteous and gave us confidence
that we will inherit eternal life.*

TITUS 3:7 NLT

You possess the God-given ability to enjoy life, because
God has rescued you from wondering what will happen
to you at the end of life. He invites you to place your

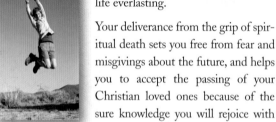

trust in his promise of salvation and
life everlasting.

Your deliverance from the grip of spiritual death sets you free from fear and
misgivings about the future, and helps
you to accept the passing of your
Christian loved ones because of the
sure knowledge you will rejoice with
them again in heaven. Just imagine the pleasure of seeing again their eyes and their smiles and hearing the
sound of their voices!

The joy of salvation is joy for today.

*Heavenly Father: Grant me the certainty of your
complete deliverance from spiritual death so I
may spend my days in joyful expectation
of the life to come in you. Amen.*

God alone is my rock and my salvation;
he is my fortress, I will never be shaken.

PSALM 62:2 NIV

EXTRAORDINARY DAYS

Happy are those who hear the joyful call to worship,
for they will walk in the light of your presence, LORD.
PSALM 89:15 NLT

When you're with someone you love, even ordinary activities take on the glow of happiness. Spend a few moments now to meditate on God's compassionate

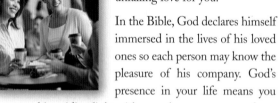 presence in your life and his unfailing love for you.

In the Bible, God declares himself immersed in the lives of his loved ones so each person may know the pleasure of his company. God's presence in your life means you carry his guiding light with you wherever you go and you can enjoy his divine companionship, even during the most mundane tasks on the most ordinary days.

Of course, in his extraordinary presence, there's no such thing as an ordinary day!

Heavenly Father: Thank you for the gift of your
presence in my life, because with you all my
days are infused with purpose and pleasure.
I delight in your companionship. Amen.

*You have upheld me because of my integrity,
and set me in your presence forever.*

PSALM 41:12 NRSV

STILLNESS IN HIM

A heart at peace gives life to the body.
PROVERBS 14:30 NIV

Spiritual peace is not simply an absence of turmoil, but an exciting and multifaceted gift God desires to nurture in your heart.

The peace he offers supplies you with the strength it takes to confront life's tumultuous changes and formidable challenges. His peace includes his other spiritual gifts of faith  and trust, wisdom, and confidence. When you accept it and let it reside within you, others cannot help but feel it, and they will be drawn to you.

Let God center his peace deep within you. When he does, you will experience the pleasure of stillness in him even during the most stressful of times.

Dear God: Open my heart to your gift of peace that comes from putting my complete trust in you, knowing I have your peace always. Amen.

The Lord will give His people peace.

PSALM **29:11** NLV

EVERYDAY WONDERS

*Christ made everything in the
heavens and on the earth.*
COLOSSIANS 1:16 NLV

A small child enthralled by the feel of grass and the sight
of wildflowers grew up to become an accomplished
nature artist.

Today, take a few moments to notice
the simple wonders of nature. Watch
clouds floating, listen to leaves rustling
in the wind, delight in the rose's fragrance and fresh-cut grass. Pick up a
pebble, twig, or shell to keep where
you'll see it every day, and let yourself
become enthralled and enchanted by
the gift of God's creation. You don't need to be an accomplished artist to see the beauty in nature. You just need to
see God's work in all the world around you.

*Creator-God: Thank you for the beauty and
magnificence of creation. Open the eyes of
my spirit to see and appreciate the
natural wonders around me
every day. Amen.*

Take a good look at God's wonders—
they'll take your breath away.

Psalm 66:5 MSG

LIFE OF PLENTY

*God will generously provide all you need. Then you
will always have everything you need and
plenty left over to share with others.*
2 CORINTHIANS 9:8 NLT

The Bible tells of a destitute widow and her son who
encountered the prophet Elijah as she was preparing a
 meal with the last of her oil and flour. A
severe famine left little hope for more.
Nevertheless, Elijah asked her the
unthinkable—use what you have left to
bake me a loaf of bread. Out of respect for
God she did as he asked and quickly found
her flour and oil containers were miracu-
lously refilled each time she ran out.

Through all the circumstances and opportunities of your
life, God sees to your needs, and he invites you to take pleasure in his provisions by sharing generously with others.

*Dear God: Allow me many opportunities to give of my
time, effort, and provisions so I may truly enjoy and
appreciate all you have given to me. Amen.*

"My people will be filled with My goodness," says the Lord.

JEREMIAH 31:14 NLV

GOD'S GOOD WILL

The world and its desires pass away, but the man
who does the will of God lives forever.
1 JOHN 2:17 NIV

"It's God's will" is a phrase often spoken with a sigh over the sadness of loss. The closer you come to understanding God's will, however, the more likely you are to

exclaim joyfully, "It's God's will!" as you consider the good things he makes happen in your life.

God, in his boundless love for you, reveals his will to you so you can make your choices and decisions in accordance with it. He urges you to learn more about his good purposes for you by studying the Bible. He wants you to follow his will and know that it is the path to true happiness.

Heavenly Father: Thank you for making
your will known to me. Grant me
wisdom that I may take pleasure in
following the good plans you
have for my life. Amen.

Teach me to do your will, for you are my God.
May your gracious Spirit lead me
forward on a firm footing.

PSALM 143:10 NLT

IN CONTROL

*It is God who is at work in you, enabling you both
to will and to work for his good pleasure.*
PHILIPPIANS 2:13 NRSV

All of us like to feel we exert some measure of control
over the events of our lives, yet it takes only one com-

pletely unexpected turn to reveal the
limits of our power and influence.

When you acknowledge God's supreme
control, you equip yourself with the perspective you need to handle those times
you must admit you have no control—
when good plans fall through, when
unforeseen trouble arises, when any
move you make to change things proves futile. When
you feel most powerless, you can smile, because God
continues to take care of and handle those things that
concern you. And he does so for your ultimate good.

*Dear God: When events move beyond my control, help
me rest in you, acknowledging my limitations and
relying on you to see me through. Amen.*

*Letting the Spirit control your mind
leads to life and peace.*

ROMANS 8:6 NLT

SWEET DREAMS

If you sit down, you will not be afraid; when you lie down, your sleep will be sweet.

PROVERBS 3:24 NRSV

The benefits of a sufficient amount of sleep include better physical health, increased mental acuity, greater emotional control, and general well-being. While the benefits are well known, few women say they regularly enjoy a good night's sleep.

God makes it possible for you to get a good night's sleep by removing those things that keep you awake. He lifts your cares from you, and he hears your words of thanksgiving for the blessings of your day, of confession for the errors of the day, and of trust in him for a fresh start tomorrow. Do this, and sleep peacefully all the hours your body and soul require.

Dear God: Help me commit to enjoying a good night's sleep by making time for sleep and closing my day with a prayer of thanksgiving, confession, and trust. Amen.

*I will lie down and sleep in peace,
O Lord, You alone keep me safe.*

PSALM 4:8 NLV

FOUNTAIN OF YOUTH

Put on your new nature, and be renewed as you learn to know your Creator and become like him.
COLOSSIANS 3:10 NLT

Noticing the first gray hair or confronting a few laugh lines in the mirror, we acknowledge, usually with a sigh,

we're not getting any younger. At the same time, God restores, renews, and rejuvenates our spiritual selves through the work of his Spirit within us.

Because of your faith, God continually restores your relationship with him by offering you absolute forgiveness. In your soul, God's Spirit renews your commitment to follow him and rejuvenates your faith, empowering you to overcome challenges and obstacles along the way.

Relax and enjoy God's antidote for aging—restoration, renewal, and rejuvenation in him.

Dear God: I need the spiritual refreshment you offer through faith, forgiveness, and commitment to follow you through all the days and stages of my life. Amen.

We are being renewed day by day.

2 CORINTHIANS 4:16 NIV

WORTH EVERYTHING

I have called you by name; you are mine.
ISAIAH 43:1 NLT

For the daughter of migrant farmworkers, time in the classroom depended on how long her parents worked in  a particular place. She dreamed of a better life, and with the help of caring educators, she eventually earned a college degree.

Though obstacles may hinder your desire to enjoy the peace of mind God offers, to mature in faith, and to become the woman God wants you to be, God acts as your caring counselor. He is committed to seeing you become all you can be, and he sends his Spirit to convince you of his ongoing care for you.

As a daughter of God, you are worth everything to him.

Heavenly Father: Help me to see myself in your eyes as a woman precious to you, and help me respond by making my life a testament to your love. Amen.

Before I shaped you in the womb, I knew all
about you. Before you saw the light
of day, I had holy plans for you.

JEREMIAH 1:5 MSG

SWEET SOLITUDE

In quietness and confidence shall be your strength.
ISAIAH 30:15 NKJV

To find a place of stillness and soul-nurturing solitude, you do not need to plan a retreat in the woods or isolate yourself in a secluded cabin. Just look within yourself.

God's Spirit, dwelling in you, has fixed a shelter for your soul, a place of peace where you can delight in being alone with him.

Achieving a quiet heart and mind takes practice, as anyone following the contemplative life will tell you. Start with a few minutes of quiet time, focusing your thoughts on God, and then gradually add more time to your meditation. Learn to rest in his peace and enjoy the sweetness of his solitude.

Heavenly Father: Draw me ever closer
to you by teaching me how to quiet
my mind and wait in patient
attendance on you. Amen.

Be still, and know that I am God.

PSALM 46:10 NIV

GLAD PRAISE

Ascribe to the LORD the glory due his name;
worship the LORD in the splendor of his holiness.
PSALM 29:2 NIV

You make time for and look forward to an activity you truly enjoy, and God wants you to approach worship the same way. He opens the doors of his heart for you. Enter  with anticipation and expectation that he, your host, will be pleased with your praise and thanksgiving.

Visualize yourself standing in the presence of your God and King with a light heart and broad smile, soaking up his goodness, basking in his love. Allow your voice to rise in response, whether in song or with simple words, and make it your own special gift. Then make time for and look forward to your next worship opportunity.

Heavenly Father: I am grateful for all the opportunities I have to worship you, and my heart responds with gladness at the privilege of standing in your presence. Amen.

Thank him. Worship him. For god is sheer beauty,
all-generous in love, loyal always and ever.

PSALM 100:4–5 MSG

TOGETHER WITH HIM

We're telling you so you can experience it along with us, this experience of communion with the Father and his Son, Jesus Christ.
1 JOHN 1:3 MSG

When Jesus walked on earth, he demonstrated his desire to forge close and lasting bonds with his people.  Through their New Testament accounts, women and men privileged to follow him reach out to believers now, inviting all to experience the fellowship they enjoyed with him.

God's Spirit opens you to the spiritual union he yearns to establish between you and him, and he makes it possible for you to follow him. As you read through the Bible, you hear him speak on subjects of everyday life and teach on topics of eternal significance. Your fellowship with him compels you to invite others to experience the communion you have with God.

Dear God: Help me respond to your fellowship by gladly sharing my experience with others so they, too, may draw close to you. Amen.

God will do this, for he is faithful to do what he says, and he has invited you into partnership with his Son, Jesus Christ our Lord.

1 CORINTHIANS 1:9 NLT

JOY TODAY

The Spirit of God has made me; the breath
of the Almighty gives me life.
JOB 33:4 NIV

Someone once said, "To dream of the woman you would like to be in the future is to waste the woman you are right now."

The woman you are right now is a woman beloved of God, a woman he welcomes with love and compassion. He knows your heart, your thoughts, and your feelings with an intimacy beyond anyone's knowledge of you, even beyond the knowledge you have of yourself. He shares this with you so you can enjoy yourself and take pleasure in the life you live and each day he has given to you.

There's happiness in being you, because Almighty God has made you who you are.

Almighty God: Surround me with your life-giving
presence, enabling me to grasp the wonder of my life
and delight in the woman I am today. Amen.

With you, O LORD, is the fountain of life;
in your light we see light.

PSALM 36:9 NIV

Caring

HE CARES FOR YOU

Keep yourself pure.
1 TIMOTHY 5:22 NIV

You have full permission to take care of yourself, not only from health counselors, but from God.

The Bible says God created your body and gave you life,  complete with intelligence, feelings, emotions, soul, and spirit. He wants you to care for your whole person, and he offers many ways for you to do so.

You care for yourself his way when you avoid unhealthy habits of body and mind and keep yourself as physically, mentally, and spiritually fit as possible. Taking care of yourself involves time and effort, but God is pleased when you make it a priority. He wants you to be always at the "top of your game."

Creator-God: Thank you for your eternal loving care for me. Grant me a heart ready to do those things I need to do for my own physical, emotional, and spiritual well-being. Amen.

*I shall yet praise him, who is the health of
my countenance, and my God.*

PSALM 43:5 KJV

FAMILY TIES

A wise woman strengthens her family.
PROVERBS 14:1 NCV

At some point in life, many women find themselves in the role of sole or contributing caregiver for children, parents, or other relatives.

When you respond willingly and wholeheartedly to the needs of your family members, you are following God's plan for families—that is, a group of people devoted to helping, encouraging, and nurturing one another, and who create a safe, comfortable, and nurturing environment for everyone.

Your status as daughter, wife, mother, aunt, or grandmother offers you the privilege and opportunity to strengthen the bonds between the people in your family. Your relationship with God inspires you to do so with joy and gladness.

Dear God: Grant me a generous heart and willing hands to care for the members of my family. Help me find ways to enrich and strengthen our bonds. Amen.

*It takes wisdom to have a good family, and it takes
understanding to make it strong.*

PROVERBS 24:3 NCV

TREASURES OF THE HEART

*In everything you do, put God first, and he will
direct you and crown your efforts with success.*

PROVERBS 3:6 TLB

The woman placed her grandmother's porcelain tray in
her china cabinet alongside a glass figurine she bought
on a trip to Asia. She protects these treasures because

they are precious to her, and
she enjoys looking at them.

The forefront of your heart is
like a spiritual china cabinet
where you place your most
cherished hopes, dreams,
memories, and desires. You
look at them often, and you

take hold of every opportunity to bring them into your
life.

God sees the things you cherish, and he knows their
intrinsic quality and eternal value. He invites you to talk
with him about the treasures he prizes above all else.

*Heavenly Father: Look into my heart and help me
choose to cherish those things you care about and
those things you hold above all others. Amen.*

*Take delight in the LORD, and he will give
you the desires of your heart.*

PSALM 37:4 NRSV

PERSONAL TOUCH

A gracious woman retains honor.

PROVERBS 11:16 NKJV

You know how good it feels when someone you've met only briefly calls you by name, or a friend remembers an event important to you. These kindnesses require time and effort but are guaranteed to bring joy to others and a sense of grace to your life.

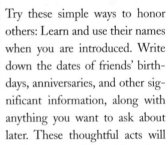

Try these simple ways to honor others: Learn and use their names when you are introduced. Write down the dates of friends' birthdays, anniversaries, and other significant information, along with anything you want to ask about later. These thoughtful acts will give kindness a starting place in your life and let others know in a real and individual way that you care about them.

Dear God: Just as you know me by name, empower me with a genuine desire to treat others as the unique individuals they are and to show I care about them. Amen.

Love is patient. Love is kind.

1 Corinthians 13:4 NIrV

JUST MEANS TO AN END

Defend the rights of the poor and needy.
PROVERBS 31:9 NIV

The history of women and their role in society makes us especially attuned to the plight of those who find themselves powerless because of factors beyond their control, such as age, gender, ethnicity, or economic status.

 You help loose the bonds of injustice when you take a firm stand against it, beginning with the opinions you harbor, the conversations you join, and the way you treat weak and vulnerable people. You continue by volunteering in your community and pledging your support to responsible charities.

God loves the poor and needy, regardless of how they became so. He wants to use your hands and heart to convey his love and concern.

Dear God: Thank you for allowing me to reflect your care for the needy through the things I can do for those who struggle against injustice. Amen.

*A good woman is hard to find.... She's quick to
assist anyone in need, reaches out to help the poor.*

PROVERBS 31:10, 20 MSG

LIVING WELL

*Let each of you look not to your own interests,
but to the interests of others.*

PHILIPPIANS 2:4 NRSV

If you're in the working world, you've probably been advised to look out for your own interests first, because no one else will. If you've been following God's way, for

even a short time, however, you already know he turns the advice upside down and says, "Put the interests of others before your own."

God's Spirit opens the way for you to consider how your decisions affect others and whether or not you want to carry out a par-

ticular plan, given the consequences your actions are likely to have on the lives of others.

Not everyone will understand why you don't put yourself first, but God will.

*Dear God: Help me turn my attention to others, keeping
in mind the consequences my words and actions
have on the lives of those around me. Amen.*

Love isn't selfish.

1 CORINTHIANS 13:5 CEV

MENDING WOUNDS

The LORD ... has sent me to bring good news to the
oppressed, to bind up the brokenhearted.

ISAIAH 61:1 NRSV

"If I can stop one heart from breaking," Emily
Dickinson wrote, "I shall not live in vain."

The poet knew that the key to a
rewarding life is to focus not on our
own comfort but on the comfort and
happiness of others. Each day you
"stop one heart from breaking" by
listening attentively to the voice of
another, hearing what that one says,
and being sensitive to those things
only suggested in a look, a shrug, or a sigh. Your willingness to empathize and extend yourself on the behalf of
another, even at the price of inconvenience to you, guarantees you "shall not live in vain."

Dear God: Grant me a heart like yours—filled with
compassion and always ready to receive those who weep
and whose spirits cry out for consolation. Amen.

God heals the brokenhearted.

PSALM 147:3 NCV

GOOD NEIGHBOR POLICY

Love your neighbor as yourself.

LEVITICUS 19:18 NIV

We're right to react with compassion, even anger, when we hear about third-world women and their children living in abject poverty, yet we often find ourselves immune to the many kinds of suffering endured by people living in our own communities.

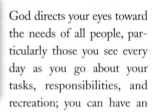

God directs your eyes toward the needs of all people, particularly those you see every day as you go about your tasks, responsibilities, and recreation; you can have an immediate and a visible impact on the lives and well-being of your closest neighbors. Your nonjudgmental assistance and your willingness to extend yourself for the sake of making their lives better places you on the path to true happiness.

Heavenly Father: Teach me to see others as you see them so I will do everything in my power to help them, encourage them, and forge productive and harmonious relationships. Amen.

Never walk away from someone who deserves help; your hand is God's hand for that person.

PROVERBS 3:28 MSG

GOD'S FAMILY

*Encourage the oppressed. Defend the cause of the
fatherless, plead the case of the widow.*

ISAIAH 1:17 NIV

"She has no one but me to help her," the woman said,
"and I'm afraid I'll end up the same way." The single

woman pictured herself
alone and helpless, but she
was forgetting one undeni-
able fact—she belonged to
God's family.

Your relationship with God
puts you in direct relation-
ship with others who love him. With the privilege of
relationship comes the responsibility to be sensitive to
the needs of those in your circle. The same is true for
your friends in the faith, for in your time of need you
have not only the right but the obligation to ask them to
help you. It's what family is for.

*Dear God: Motivate me to help those in my faith
family who need assistance, and help me to be
willing to reach out to others in my own
time of need. Amen.*

Whenever we have an opportunity, let us work for the good of all, and especially for those of the family of faith.

GALATIANS 6:10 NRSV

FAITH-FULL FINANCES

He who gathers money little by little makes it grow.
PROVERBS 13:11 NIV

During Jesus' earthly ministry, a number of women regularly provided provisions for him and his disciples. Those women now serve as an example to us of how to use financial resources in an unselfish and God-honoring way.

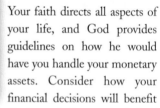

Your faith directs all aspects of your life, and God provides guidelines on how he would have you handle your monetary assets. Consider how your financial decisions will benefit and bring goodness into the lives of others, and ask God for his wisdom and discernment.

Whether you possess a large investment portfolio or only some change at the bottom of your purse, care for your money as the gift of God it is.

Dear God: Teach me to use my God-given financial resources in a responsible manner that honors you and to see to the needs of others before my own. Amen.

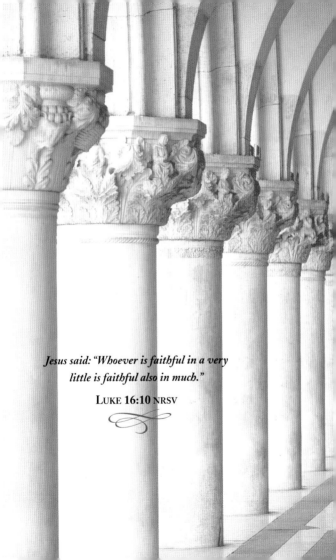

Jesus said: "Whoever is faithful in a very little is faithful also in much."

LUKE 16:10 NRSV

GODLY BUSINESS

*A faithful employee is as refreshing as a cool
day in the hot summertime.*

PROVERBS 25:13 TLB

Every day you might deal with bosses, clients,
customers, staff members, assistants. Even if your
work is in your home, you may encounter others as you
carry out your daily routine. God
challenges you to take the lead in
building and maintaining God-
pleasing work relationships.

Choose to respect others, seeing
them as women and men God loves,
and treat them with kindness and
compassion. Remember them in your
prayers, taking their needs to God
and asking him how you can serve and support them as
they go about their duties and responsibilities. Bring
God's Spirit into every business relationship; show genuine care for those God has placed in your life.

*Heavenly Father: Help me become an instrument of your
love and compassion for others as I go about the
business of my day. Let me remember that in
all things, I report to you. Amen.*

…t the loveliness of our Lord, our God, rest on us,
confirming the work that we do.

PSALM 90:17 MSG

HEART OF COMPASSION

Honor God by accepting each other,
as Christ has accepted you.

ROMANS 15:7 CEV

From your school days, you may remember the one little girl no one seemed to like, and even today you may be able to name a woman spurned by others for

obvious reasons, or for no discernible reason at all.

God asks of you a heart of compassion for the person others shun, for this is the kind of person Jesus made a point to speak to and to

whom he extended his merciful, healing touch. With a welcoming smile, a kind word, and thoughtful gestures, you bring God's love to people he cares about, people perhaps not readily accepted by others, but like you, precious in his sight.

Dear God: Grant me a compassionate heart and enable
me to reach out to those whom others shun, so all may
know of your deep love for every soul on earth. Amen.

Be imitators of God as dear children. And walk in love, as Christ also has loved us.

EPHESIANS 5:1–2 NKJV

LIFTED VOICE

Speak up for those who cannot speak for themselves,
for the rights of all who are destitute.

The New Testament tells the story of Jesus encountering a funeral procession. The grieving widow had lost her only son. Jesus touched the boy and restored his life. In

bringing the son back to his anguished mother, he also restored her dignity and her livelihood. Without a male family member to provide for her, she would have faced a life of destitution.

Today, young children, special-needs adults, and the elderly rely on others to care for and about them. God appeals to people to willingly and faithfully see to others' well-being. He calls you to speak out for those who lack the voice or clout to be heard, and to see to their needs.

Heavenly Father: Grant me the courage to lift up
my voice on behalf of those who lack strength,
power, or resources to make their needs
and wants known. Amen.

Blessed is the person who is kind to those in need.

PROVERBS 14:21 NIrV

CREATED FOR YOUR PLEASURE

God spoke: "Let us make human beings in our image, make them reflecting our nature So they can be responsible for the fish in the sea, the birds in the air, the cattle, And, yes, Earth itself."

GENESIS 1:26 MSG

Environmentalism has emerged as a topic for debate among political leaders, activists, and conservationists, but God had something to say about environmentalism at the time he spoke the world into existence. He gave

humankind the privilege of being the crown of his creation and the responsibility of caring for his creation.

Let your gratitude for the world God fashioned prompt you to take a lively interest in issues surrounding clean air, soil, and water—gifts both to you and to generations to come. Show your respect for him by dealing kindly with all the living creatures of land, sea, and sky.

Creator-God: You have created a place of beauty and a resource for food and water. Enable me to do my part in protecting the world you have made. Amen.

The Lord is the eternal God, Creator of the earth.

Isaiah **40:28** CEV

Sharing

MUTUAL FEELINGS

*All of you be of one mind, having
compassion for one another.*
1 Peter 3:8 nkjv

Compassion is a wonderful thing. By an act of your will,
you enter into another person's pain, sorrow, or sadness.
You help shoulder the load. That's what God did when

he had compassion toward you.
He came down to where you
were. He took your pain and
sorrow and suffering on himself.
That's what true compassion is
all about.

Two things happen when you
show compassion for others: You
find yourself feeling good because God created you to
find fulfillment helping others—you find it every time
you extend a hand to someone in need. You also open
yourself up to receive the compassion others extend
when you need it.

*Dear God: Increase my willingness to act with
compassion toward others, and open my heart
to receive with joy and gratitude the care
and comfort others lavish on me. Amen.*

*Are your hearts tender and compassionate?
Then make me truly happy by agreeing
wholeheartedly with each other, loving
one another, and working together
with one mind and purpose.*

PHILIPPIANS 2:1–2 NLT

A LIGHTER LOAD

*God comforts us every time we have trouble, so
when others have trouble, we can comfort them
with the same comfort God gives us.*

2 CORINTHIANS 1:4 NCV

Declaring "I don't want to get involved" or "I don't know
what to say," some women avoid a troubled acquaintance

or pass by a sorrowing friend. We've
all done that at one time or another.

The next time someone needs comfort and you don't know how to help,
stop and pray. Ask God to comfort
that person just as he has comforted
you in times of sadness and sorrow.
Ask his Holy Spirit to make his love
and compassion real to her. Then ask
what you can do to help. You can be confident that God
knows best, and he will show you what to do to be a
blessing.

*God of Comfort: Just as I find my solace in you,
empower me through your Spirit to ease the
sorrows of others by bringing to them
the comfort of your love. Amen.*

"Comfort, comfort my people," says your God.

ISAIAH 40:1 NLT

HELP WITH HEAVY LIFTING

Share each other's troubles and problems,
and so obey our Lord's command.
GALATIANS 6:2 TLB

Most of us would ask for help lifting a one-hundred-pound trunk, but we avoid getting help with heavy burdens of heart and spirit. God never intends for us to bear

problems and troubles by ourselves. That's why he places us among others—friends and family—so not one of us needs to stumble under a full load.

Think of the women you know and consider the many unique skills and abilities they represent.

Don't forget to include your own. Count up their backgrounds, experiences, and gifts, and you will realize you're among heavy lifters who can assist one another with heart-heavy burdens of all kinds.

Together you can move mountains.

Heavenly Father: By your Spirit, make me a willing
sharer of others' burdens, and give me the grace to ask my
friends for help with my troubles and problems. Amen.

Jesus said: "Come to Me, all who are weary and heavy-laden, and I will give you rest.

MATTHEW 11:28 NASB

GOING FORWARD

Encourage each other every day while it is "today."
HEBREWS 3:13 NCV

Women who occupy the top echelons of a corporation, who win awards for achievements in athletics or the arts, or who have achieved great things in society often attribute their success to someone who urged them to persevere until they reached their goal.

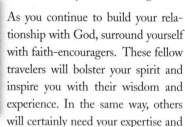

As you continue to build your relationship with God, surround yourself with faith-encouragers. These fellow travelers will bolster your spirit and inspire you with their wisdom and experience. In the same way, others will certainly need your expertise and insight to urge them ahead as they mature in the faith.

God would have you generously give and gladly receive encouragement as you persevere in your walk of faith.

*Dear God: I thank you for the encouragement
I receive from those around me. Help
me to be an encouragement
to others. Amen.*

We pray that our Lord Jesus Christ and God our Father will encourage you and help you always to do and say the right thing.

2 THESSALONIANS 2:16–17 CEV

WISE WOMAN'S WORDS

*The quiet words of the wise are more to be heeded
than the shouting of a ruler among fools.*
ECCLESIASTES 9:17 NRSV

Remember the last time someone offered you meaningful words of advice, and the way the advice was given? In all likelihood, your friend spoke in a calm, thoughtful  manner, and because she was gentle, you benefited from her knowledge and experience in a positive way.

When you believe your knowledge could help another person or your experience could save her from a mistake, share your insight in a kindly and affirming way. Sensitive subjects can be awkward and even embarrassing, but consider that your silence could cause the greater hurt.

Use your wisdom—your lessons learned, your failings overcome—to lift up others. It is the loving thing to do.

*God of All Wisdom: Grant me wisdom to know when to
share my thoughts with others, and put in my mouth
words of true helpfulness and spiritual insight. Amen.*

All wisdom comes from the LORD, and so do common sense and understanding.

PROVERBS 2:6 CEV

TRUTH TALKS

Love should always make us tell the truth.
Then we will grow in every way and be
more like Christ, the head of the body.
EPHESIANS 4:15–16 CEV

A friend excitedly relates her latest news, and you recognize it as something that could cause her future pain and

sadness. Have you ever found yourself in this predicament? What do you say?

The Bible teaches us that real love always tells the truth. And you've probably already learned that offenses most often come not from what we say but from how we say it. Ask God to prepare your heart, wiping away any ulterior motives, pride, or judgmental attitudes. Ask him to make you his instrument of loving truth. Your courage could save a friend from a good deal of heartache.

Dear God: Grant me the courage and confidence I
need to tell the truth in a world so much in
need of your guidance, and help me
always to speak in love. Amen.

The Lord is pleased with people who tell the truth.

PROVERBS 12:22 NIrV

FOREVER FRIENDS

Jesus said, "Greater love has no one than this,
than to lay down one's life for his friends.
JOHN 15:13 NKJV

Friendship has been called a plant requiring constant care, and indeed, the delightful flowers of friendship bloom only with our commitment to faithfully nurture those relationships.

By willingly giving his life, Jesus forged a bond of eternal friendship between God and you, and his sacrifice provides an example for all his disciples to follow. He has shown you how to give of yourself to your friends by generously offering them your time and companionship, and willingly providing to each of them your unconditional love. Jesus has proven the fragrance of true friendship comes not in taking from but in giving to your friends.

Dear God: Renew in me a commitment to give of myself
to my friends and do all within my power to nurture
and strengthen my friendships. Amen.

The sweet smell of incense can make you feel good,
but true friendship is better still.

PROVERBS 27:9 CEV

GIFTED GROUP

There are different kinds of gifts, but the same Spirit. There are different kinds of service, but the same Lord.
1 CORINTHIANS 12:4–5 NIV

God invites us to value the diverse skills and talents of others. This clearly implies the presence of at least one skill or one talent in each of us to be used for the good of all.

God's gifts to you may be obvious, and if so, he urges you to develop and broaden your talents so you can grow even more effective and productive in your given work. If you think God has left you off his gift list, think again. Consider what you do for the sake of other people, and name these things as your talents—then share them with all your heart.

Heavenly Father: Help me discover and embrace the unique gifts you have seen fit to give me that I may use my talents in joyful service to others. Amen.

Every desirable and beneficial gift comes out of heaven. The gifts are rivers of light cascading down from the Father of Light.

JAMES 1:17 MSG

WARMTH OF WELCOME

*Do not neglect to show hospitality to strangers, for by doing
that some have entertained angels without knowing it.*
HEBREWS 13:2 NRSV

The Bible tells us that the apostle Paul went to the river-
bank outside the city of Philippi one day, and he spoke
to a group of women who met there to pray. One, the

merchant Lydia, enthusiastically
embraced Paul's message, then
opened her home to Paul and his
traveling companions. We can learn
from Lydia's example.

When you invite God into your life,
his Spirit opens the door of your heart
to others, showing you how to express

hospitality through the warmth of your welcoming smile,
the provisions of your busy kitchen, the gift of your undi-
vided attention to each visitor.

Remember Lydia, and consider all the ways you can
open your home and your heart to others.

*Heavenly Father: Inspire in me the gift of hospitality so I
may, both inside and outside my home, offer a welcome
that is pleasing to you. Amen.*

Be inventive in hospitality

ROMANS 12:12 MSG

GOD TALK

God abides in those who confess that Jesus is the
Son of God, and they abide in God.
1 JOHN 4:15 NRSV

One woman of faith concludes her e-mails with the words "Have a great day in Jesus." Another believing woman sprinkles her conversations with "God willing"

and "Praise God!" These phrases invite God into the conversation and give joyful witness to his presence.

Casual references to your faith in God give you opportunities to share your beliefs with another person, because his name coming reverently from your lips establishes you as either a fellow-believer in whom another can confide, or a source of information for someone who has questions.

You naturally talk about what's important to you, and it's natural for you to talk about God.

Dear God: Grant me boldness in speaking about you
and the faith you have planted in my heart. I want
to become a winsome witness to others. Amen.

You are the light of the world.... Let your light shine before others, so that they may see your good works and give glory to your Father in heaven.

MATTHEW 5:14, 16 NRSV

TRUE POSSESSING

Jesus said, "Live generously and graciously toward others, the way God lives toward you."
MATTHEW 5:48 MSG

"Here, use mine for as long as you need it," she said, handing her roommate a coat from her closet. She knew a tight budget restricted her roommate's spending, and

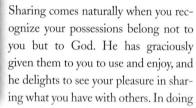

the coat would get her through the winter.

Sharing comes naturally when you recognize your possessions belong not to you but to God. He has graciously given them to you to use and enjoy, and he delights to see your pleasure in sharing what you have with others. In doing so, you develop generosity and prevent your possessions from possessing you. You also become a partner with God by helping him answer someone else's prayer and fill someone else's need.

Heavenly Father: All I have comes from you.
Help me develop a spirit of generosity and
sharing with others so I may become
more like you. Amen.

God will make you rich in every way so that you can always give freely.

2 CORINTHIANS 9:11 NCV

TIMELY MATTER

A wise heart knows the proper time and procedure.
For there is a proper time and procedure
for every delight.
ECCLESIASTES 8:5–6 NASB

As we mature, we come to realize how quickly days melt into years. We recognize time as our most precious  gift—the gift God tells us to willingly and generously share with others.

The hours you spend taking care of your family, working to provide for them, visiting the sick, comforting your friends, and helping the needy please your heavenly Father. He delights when you take time for yourself to rest and be revived in him, to keep your spiritual fire burning inside.

God-pleasing and productive sharing won't slow down the passage of time, but it will lift up your spirits and leave you with a treasure chest of heartwarming memories.

Dear God: Thank you for the days and years of my life.
Bless the time I share with others so it will bring about
happiness, encouragement, and peace. Amen.

Behold, now is the accepted time; behold, now is the day of salvation.

ECCLESIASTES 8:5–6 NASB

MANY HANDS, LIGHT WORK

Be strong and do not lose courage,
for there is reward for your work.
2 CHRONICLES 15:7 NASB

Ask for volunteers, and the same hands go up every time! Consider making your hand one of those raised when work needs to get done.

You have specific skills and special know-how needed in your home, at your workplace, in your community, and God calls you to willingly and gladly share your expertise with others. When you take on any task within your power to perform, you not only lighten the load for others who help, you receive the satisfaction of sharing your abilities, and serve as a compelling example for women who do not yet know the joy of responding to a call for help.

Dear God: Increase in me the desire to share
my skills with others, and grant me a
willingness to step forward to help
in whatever way I can. Amen.

*My heart took delight in all my work, and
this was the reward for all my labor.*

ECCLESIASTES 2:10 NIV

CELEBRATION OF BLESSINGS

The faithful will abound with blessings.
PROVERBS 28:20 NRSV

When we are hesitant to join with others in joyful celebration of God's blessings, we are like the "wallflower" at the dance; too shy to step out of the shadows onto the dance floor.

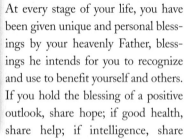

At every stage of your life, you have been given unique and personal blessings by your heavenly Father, blessings he intends for you to recognize and use to benefit yourself and others. If you hold the blessing of a positive outlook, share hope; if good health, share help; if intelligence, share insight; if curiosity, discover more about God's goodness and tell others what you found.

Celebrate your blessings by stepping out of the shadows and sharing with others.

Dear God: I come to you in humble thanks for the blessings I have received. Teach me how to share with others your goodness to me. Amen.

Blessed shall you be when you come in,
and blessed shall you be when you go out.

DEUTERONOMY 28:6 NASB

SHARE A PRAYER

*While they are still talking about their needs, I will
go ahead and answer their prayers.*
ISAIAH 65:24 NLT

The telephone rang. "I'm calling to ask for your prayers,"
the caller said, then proceeded to explain that the husband of a co-worker was undergoing surgery.

God offers you the privilege and
the power to pray for the needs of
your family, friends, and associates, in addition to the needs of
individuals or groups brought to
your attention by word of mouth
or through the media.

Share your prayers by pleading the cause of others, and
let the sound of your voice come before the throne of
God your heavenly Father, who has promised to hear the
prayers of every believing heart.

*Heavenly Father: I come before you with
the needs of others on my heart, and
I pray you will look compassionately
on them and console them
in their distress. Amen.*

"Call to me in times of trouble. I will save you,
and you will honor me," declares the LORD.

PSALM 50:15 NCV

WHAT GOES AROUND

Always try to do good to each other.
1 THESSALONIANS 5:15 NLT

Have you noticed it is often easier to extend kindness to others than to accept kindness? You've been sick for days and a friend offers to bring you some warm, nourishing  comfort food. But you say, "Oh no, I'm fine." In your effort not to inconvenience the other person, you block the blessing such kindness can bring for both of you.

God often chooses to love and care for us through others, so be quick to receive the loving care he offers and be grateful for the hands that bring it. You can be sure that he blesses them richly for their trouble. Always say "yes" to a kindness extended.

Dear God: In your Spirit, enable me
to freely receive the kindnesses
others extend, remembering
that they will be blessed
as well. Amen.

Be kindly affectionate to one another with brotherly love, in honor giving preference to one another.

ROMANS 12:10 NKJV

CONGRATULATIONS IN ORDER

The humble will see their God at work and be glad.
PSALM 69:32 NLT

To avoid the appearance of bragging, many of us keep quiet about our successes and accomplishments. Such modesty, however, robs us of the joy of sharing our happiness, and takes from others the chance to offer their congratulations and praise.

Your successes are an opportunity to invite friends to celebrate with you, giving thanks to God for his goodness in your life. Your joy may prompt them to reflect on his work in their lives, an opening God's Spirit may use to draw them closer to him and strengthen their faith.

When you have reason to celebrate, share the news about what God has done through you and rejoice with others.

Dear God: Thank you for giving me many reasons to celebrate. Let me use each occasion to spread the word of your wonderful ways. Amen.

A cheerful look brings joy to the heart;
good news makes for good health.

PROVERBS 15:30 NLT

JOY TO SHARE

Celebrate God all day, every day.
I mean, revel in him!
PHILIPPIANS 4:4 MSG

Throughout these pages, you have reflected on many aspects of the Christian journey, and now God's Spirit invites you to receive a gift for every step along the way—joy so abundant you cannot contain it within yourself.

God-given joy overflows your heart and shows in your appreciation for life, your gratitude for God's blessings, and your trust in his forgiveness, protection, and care. In the things you do and say each day, the joy of your heart shines through to others, and the serenity of your soul touches the world with his peace.

Open your arms and lavish others with your gift of abundant joy.

Heavenly Father: Lead me to receive your precious
gift with gratitude, sharing the riches of your
joy with others as you so graciously share
yourself with me. Amen.

*Yes, the LORD has done amazing
things for us! What joy!*

PSALM **126:3** NLT

May the LORD be good to you and give you peace.

NUMBERS 6:26 CEV